Through the Deep Woods

Holding My Heavenly Father's Hand

Stories of Walking with God Through Life's Trials

By

Kay Marie Bjerke

PublishAmerica
Baltimore

First printing

ISBN: 1-4137-5273-X
PUBLISHED BY PUBLISHAMERICA, LLLP
www.publishamerica.com
Baltimore

Printed in the United States of America

Permissions

Picture of Leah Nelsen was taken by KenMar Photgraphy, Appleton, WI. Used with permission.

Author Picture was taken by Robin Heil-Kern of KJ's Photo, Hudson, WI.

Beware of Practice Atheism used with permission from Creative Communications, Fenton, MO.

Dedication

I primarily dedicate this book to my Heavenly Father without whom I could well have been lost in the "Deep Woods" of life. His grace and mercy are endless.

I also dedicate this book to my husband and four children. They will all find themselves among these pages. I love them for being the special people that they have become. I thank my daughter-in-law for saying "yes" to my son and then for giving us our first-born grandchild who lights up our lives with a fresh, new spirit. I appreciate every one of them and treasure their cooperation and their support.

Dear Joan
God's love is always
with you! Kay Bjerke

Back row: sons, Brian and Kevin and husband, Cyrus. Front row: Kay Marie; daughter-in-law, Brenda, holding Taylor, and standing next to them is our daughter, Kimberly.

Table of Contents

Acknowledgments

I wish to express my heartfelt appreciation to those dear people who have shared their stories with me and consequently with you, the reader. They have unselfishly given their time to bring testimony to how our God has been with them and led them through their "Deep Woods." My love and sincere gratitude goes to each one of you!

I want to acknowledge the advice, editing work, and encouragement that Susan Erickson so willing gave me to make this book a reality.

Preface

This is a book of many stories rather than just one. All the stories are testimonies about facing a challenge or tragedy by ultimately trusting God for the strength to live day-by-day, holding His hand. I hesitated writing this book because so many of you have suffered much more in your lives than I. You may have experienced tragedy after tragedy, layering grief upon grief. You have stories of struggle, fear, and living day-by-day that we should all hear. You can give testimony of faith challenges, growth, and triumph that can inspire anyone who will listen. So, I talked to some dear friends who were willing to share their "Deep Woods" journeys with you in this book.

My hope and prayer is that this book can encourage you to share your stories with others who may need to hear them. Tragedy is a part of our common journey on earth. By sharing we can encourage one another, and we can walk forward together with faith and hope for our remaining days.

Introduction

The farm of my childhood was 120 acres of rolling hills in western Wisconsin. Our barn was tall and red with the wood stave silo; the house was a typical white two story; and several other buildings occupied the rest of the yard. It was basically a dairy farm. We raised cows, usually chickens and sometimes hogs. The crops of alfalfa, grain and corn were grown to feed our herd of dairy cows – their milk was our major source of income.

There were pastures where the cows spent the days grazing lazily in the spring, summer and autumn months. Bordering the pasture to the west was a very dense woods. We called it the "Deep Woods." It had a fence around it so the cows wouldn't wander into it and get lost. Every autumn Daddy would hook the trailer to the tractor, load up his chain saw and ax and go to the "Deep Woods" to cut firewood for burning in our furnace, which worked night and day in the long, cold winter to keep us warm. In the spring he would tap maple trees for the sap that would be boiled and boiled to become delicious maple syrup.

When I was a child, the "Deep Woods" was beautiful, mysterious and sometimes scary. It had oak, maple and elm trees standing very close together with their branches reaching high for sunlight. Thick underbrush made it hard for me to walk through. Here and there would be a little path made by the animals and enlarged by my father's occasional activities. It was one of those places, we were told, where a person could easily lose their sense of direction and end up walking in circles attempting to find a way out. I used to think about that, and it frightened me. I could just imagine not being able to find my way out and even worse, not being found. I would just have to stay in the deep woods forever.

It was also a place of many strange sounds with the cracking and creaking of the branches, and the ominous sounds of the small creatures that were at home in the woods. Squirrels would constantly jump from branch to branch; I would wonder how there could be so many squirrels. Chipmunks, gophers and even deer shared the turf. Many kinds of birds nested in the trees and sang their heavenly songs.

It was always sort of dark there – even in the daytime and, especially in the summertime when the leaves shaded everything. Nature's great and colorful leaf umbrella made the woods seem cool. We thought it was fun to find a clearing where the sun could beam through like a spotlight bringing warmth to the soil and inviting us to relax and play. But the deep woods was not a place for children to play alone. In fact, my mother gave us a stern warning, "Do not go into the Deep Woods alone! You can only go there if you hold your father's hand." I was always amazed by how Daddy never seemed to get lost. He could always find his way out by finding the trail or the path that led us out to the pasture. When we went with him, we weren't afraid.

Our "Deep Woods" taught me, as a very young child, about holding my father's hand. When I grew older, it became an analogy about holding my Heavenly Father's hand through my journey here on earth. Since I was blessed with a kind and loving earthly father, I could relate to the concept of holding my Heavenly Father's hand.

I can understand how the idea of holding your Heavenly Father's hand can be very hard to grasp if you grew up in a home without a father or with a father who was abusive and did not know how to love you. In fact, the thought may even be repulsive to you. However, there is a father who loves you, unconditionally, with all the love that actually sent His Son to the cross. I pray that this analogy will not keep you from reading this book and from being blessed by it. I am sure we can agree that there is a real security in knowing that someone is offering a hand to us to hold – a hand that can keep us from getting lost and from feeling lonely. I can never claim to know the heartache of a home without a God-fearing father; nevertheless, I would like to help you to experience that love through God. Picture a hand, and it belongs to God. God's outstretched hand is reaching to you, beckoning you to take hold of it, to feel the security of holding it, to trust that it will not let you go. You reach out now; you timidly touch the fingertips, and then you trust a little more – soon you are grasping the whole hand; and God is promising to never let your hand go.

In his book I will be sharing with you how God's hand is always outstretched. Sometimes we take it, and sometimes we try to do things our way. Sometimes we reach in absolute desperation to grasp God's hand, seeking an answer to the despair we feel in our hearts. We may know that we are in danger of getting lost in the "Deep Woods" of our life. We need help; we need guidance; we need a feeling of security; and we need to know that someone cares and someone loves us beyond our own comprehension even when we are feeling as though we are totally unlovable. Other times, decisions have us confused. Which path do I take? Which obstacle can I remove? Which can I go around? Which do I simply have to learn to live with? There are times in all of our lives when we find ourselves in a "Deep Woods" that we are trying to find our way through. Circumstances have come upon us that have darkened our lives so that our bodies and our spirits become exhausted. We haven't asked to be there, but somehow we have found ourselves smack dab in the middle of a situation where there seems to be no right answer. We know that we need help desperately – help beyond what even our best friend on this earth can give us.

The deepest of all "Woods" which we all find ourselves in many times during our earthly journey is that of grief. This may be the most difficult darkness to find our way through. We usually associate grief with death, and that certainly is profound. However, grief comes with any kind of loss: the loss of things, the loss of our place in life, the loss of trust with family members or friends, the loss of physical health, the loss of self esteem. The list goes on. Grief often comes quickly; our heads spin; our hearts are broken in a million pieces; and loneliness envelops us.

I thank God that I have not experienced many of these griefs. I do, however, know what it is to lose a son, my parents, a brother, my in-laws, a sister-in-law, nephews, a niece, other family members and good friends. These have been the toughest times in my life.

As a child, I knew that holding my father's hand would keep me from getting hopelessly lost among the trees and the shrubs of that dark place on our farm that we called the "Deep Woods." As I grew and took on the responsibilities of adult life, I no longer lived on that farm; but then I discovered that there were other "Deep Woods" that existed. The difference between the two was that as an adult I didn't choose to go into the woods – I would just slowly or suddenly realize that's where I was. At those times my mother's loving and stern warning took on a new meaning. "Never go into the 'Deep Woods,' without holding your father's hand!"

So now I invite you to journey with me as I share some of the "Deep Woods" of my life and the lives of other special people in my life. Then find a friend and share your "Deep Woods" experiences. That is when you will receive the blessing of encouraging and praying for one another.

dw

Hold my Hand

Please hold my hand, Dear Father,
Hold on to it, oh so very tightly.
"How did I get here?" I wonder.
There is no way out that I can see.
There is darkness all around.
I feel so lost and so alone,
Is there a voice or a sound?
Where is the sun that once shone?

Now I feel your hand holding mine,
Help me to trust, help me to find
Your will, for my life this very day.
Please show me the very best way
To solve my problems, each one,
As the darkness gives in to the sun.
Hand in hand through everything
I rejoice with the birds that sing.

dw

Chapter One

The Deep Woods of Despair

"Our help is in the name of the Lord, the Maker of heaven and earth." Psalms 124:8

Angel of Love

It's 6 A.M. and the rude, shrill sound of the ringing telephone startled us from our sleep. My very first thought was of our eighteen-month-old son, Kyle, who was hospitalized again. My husband, Cy, quickly picked up the receiver and the ringing silenced. After a moment I realized that he was oddly silent.

Then I heard him hesitantly say, "You better talk to Kay."

Cy was pale as he handed me the receiver. The most dreaded words in the world pierced my heart as our pediatrician said, "I'm sorry, Mrs. Bjerke, we did all that we could; but it just wasn't enough this time. Kyle died a few minutes ago."

I screamed back at him, "You must be mistaken! We've saved him many times before. He can't be gone."

Cy couldn't console me; I beat the wall with my fists until I was exhausted. Then out of desperation, all I wanted to do was to get to the hospital as soon as possible to prove the doctor wrong – as irrational as that was. Waking him from sleep, we hurriedly dressed our four-year-old son, Brian. We needed to have him with us; we had always been through Kyle's struggles together.

Awakened by the commotion, my brother, Dale, who was staying with us at the time, came into the room. He soon knew what had happened and began to make calls to our immediate family and friends while we three left for the hospital.

Kyle weighed nine pounds at birth. During the first eleven days of his life we rejoiced over our second, apparently healthy baby boy. Brian was two-and-a-half-years old when Kyle was born, and he was proud to be a big brother.

When Kyle was twelve days old, I could definitely tell that he was not feeling well. In the late morning, I called his pediatrician because he would stiffen his body and cry. The doctor said that he was experiencing some stomach problems that would pass. However, Kyle didn't get better and in the afternoon when I called the doctor again, he suggested that if he wasn't better by the next day I should bring him into the office.

The day was Maundy Thursday, and Cy was scheduled to usher at church that night. Soon after he left, Kyle had a very bad spell. I called the doctor and told him that I was not waiting until the next day, but that I was bringing him to the emergency room immediately! He assured me that he would meet us there. A neighbor drove us so that I could cuddle Kyle in the car. After an examination, it was determined that Kyle was actually experiencing seizures. It would be necessary to keep him overnight to observe him and determine which course of care should be taken. It was really tough to leave him there. Staying over with your children wasn't even an option in 1972. It was a relief to bring him to the ER because I trusted that we would get help for him. When we needed to admit our brand-new baby son to the hospital and leave him in this sterile place full of strangers, in a crib where lots of other babies had been, and where my arms could not cuddle him – it just seemed like such a cold and such a lonely place for the tiny child we loved so much. I remember going to the elevator and dreading to get on it and go home without him.

The morning was actually on Good Friday. We went to the hospital as soon as we could and learned that the results of several tests concluded that Kyle was suffering from a major brain hemorrhage. The doctor gave him a slim chance of pulling through this crises. Our Pastor from Our Saviour's Lutheran Church in Minneapolis came to the hospital as did Kyle's two aunts and two uncles, who became Godparents; and Kyle was Baptized right there in his room.

He was kept sedated so that there would be a better chance for the healing to proceed. To everyone's surprise and our tremendous relief, Easter Sunday brought a report that was slightly positive.

The blood that was in his spinal fluid, because of the bleeding in his brain, eventually disappeared; and we were assured that the hemorrhage had indeed healed. (The cause was not known; it was only assumed that it was caused from an aneurysm.) It was great news, and we started anticipating the day when we could once again take our baby son home.

That homecoming, however, was still several weeks away. One day when I came to the hospital, the doctor asked me if I noticed anything different about the way Kyle's face and head were looking. I replied that it seemed his skin was a little tighter and his head was a little bigger. We were told then that Kyle had developed hydrocephalus, more commonly known as water on the brain. After consultations with a neurosurgeon, he was scheduled for brain surgery. A shunt (tube) was inserted from a ventricle in his brain into the jugular vein to drain off excess fluid. It worked and I was trained to pump the shunt twice a day by pressing on it three times at a particular spot behind his right ear. It was evidently a rather rare occurrence because I, in turn, had to train some of the nurses on how to take care of his shunt. Eventually, we saw improvement in his appearance and alertness. However, there were many unanswered questions that only time would resolve. We had no idea of the amount of brain damage that may have occurred at the time of the hemorrhage.

Six long weeks after his hospitalization the much anticipated homecoming day arrived. Words fail to express the gratefulness that exciting day brought. Once again he could sleep in his crib in the room he shared with Brian. The time-consuming, daily trips to the hospital had ended, and we could resume more normal days as a family.

Kyle did grow and was very alert, but it became apparent that the motor functions on his right side were impaired. The thumb and fingers on that hand did not move independently; so, he had to wear a little brace. When he was old enough to start sitting, he would slump to the right side. At nine months he started physical therapy at the Sister Kinney Institute in Minneapolis. We were taught how to exercise his limbs at home. With the help of medication to control seizures, he was in many ways like other nine-month-old children. He had his favorite toys he loved to play with; and "Daddy" was his first and only actual spoken word. We were given a lot of hope – even that he would one-day walk (possibly with the help of braces).

At Sister Kinney I found a support group. There were many other mothers who would bring their child several times a week for therapy; and there were children with every imaginable disability – many of them severe. Watching the therapists work with them was amazing. Every little improvement, every little achievement, every little step in the right direction was praised and celebrated. Tired, exhausted mothers would hug, and tears of joy would surface. It was a place where every bit of energy from everyone involved was put into helping the children have a better life. I became a friend with one mother in particular whose son, Bradley, had multiple disabilities. We often found ourselves on the phone with each other, comparing notes and sharing frustrations, hopes and joys. It was another world – a world of very special children.

Only people who have experienced having a child with special needs can begin to realize the intensity of the desperation there is to help that child in any way possible. One of the driving forces is fear. Fear for that child's future. Will my child ever walk? Will my child be mentally, intellectually or emotionally impaired? Will my child ever be able to give and receive love? How will my child relate to other people? How will other people relate to my child? Will my child be unjustly judged? And the most intensely burning fear of all is – will I see my child die? Then there is fear for the parents. Are we capable of handling this situation that we have found ourselves in? Will we make the correct decisions for treatment, education, therapy, and other special care that may be necessary? Will the stress be a threat to our marriage? With this child needing so much attention, will our other child/children get the attention that they need to grow up healthy and be well-adjusted individuals? Is there something else, anything else that we should be doing?

Our faith has been an important part of my husband's and my life, as individuals and as a couple. We met in church, were married in church and found a church home early in our life together. When Kyle was hospitalized, he was placed on many prayer chains and prayed for during our church's Sunday Services. A dear friend of ours came to the hospital; and we surrounded Kyle's crib, held hands and prayed. After we brought him home we continued to seek out spiritual support. We were given books to read and told about places to go for healing services. We also started going to a local non-denominational charismatic church (in addition to, not in place of, our own church). We were saturated with the message, from this church and the books that I was reading, that "it was definitely God's will that Kyle should be healed." All that was needed was anointing with oil, rebuking of Satan, and a strong enough faith particularly on the part of the mother. Wow! You mean my faith can really heal my child! So I started on the most intense spiritual journey of my life. What a responsibility for a mother to accept! We had the "laying on of hands" for Kyle. He was prayed for by this new group we were attending. I read the books, over and over. All I needed was enough faith – just enough faith. I was told to take Kyle off his seizure medication because it would be a sign that I believed that he was healed. Amazingly, he did not seizure for quite sometime. When he would have a slight symptom now and then, I was told to rebuke Satan. I was assured it was not real but just Satan trying to make us doubt. I just needed enough faith.

How much faith was enough? I began to wonder. I was trying, I was praying, I was loving; and, yet, one day it seemed to me that he actually had another seizure. Out of frustration, I called the "pastor" of that church and told him, "I am sorry. I don't know if my faith is really weak or not, but my child is not going to suffer unnecessarily; and I am not going to risk this anymore. I am putting him back on his medication." I did. I quit reading the books, and we quit going to that church.

What was happening here? I learned that God wasn't depending on the strength of my imperfect faith or my husband's (Cy) for that matter. The Bible tells us to ask for God's will not to demand from Him or tell Him what His will is to be. Oh yes, I certainly believe that physical healing can and at times does miraculously happen here on earth. I now believe that we must pray and trust God for that decision and that work. God gave Kyle to us to care for the best way we knew how, and that included making use of medication if needed. I am so thankful that I had been brought up in a Christian home and had stayed with the church throughout my younger years. I believe that gave me a foundation to hold on to during this "faith crisis." Even though I feel we were, out of the deep need to help our child, led somewhat astray – listening to "human" interpretation rather than trusting totally in God, we didn't lose our faith. Instead we relaxed and were more able to put Kyle into God's hands.

Kyle's first year was filled with therapy, lots of attention from us and a couple more hospitalizations for viruses because his natural immune system had been destroyed as a result of his first major crises. A few trips to the ER were required to unplug the shunt, but we always brought him back home. He was recognizing people, responding to us with smiles, and excitedly kicking and waving his arms. It warms my heart with joy when I recall how Brian could make him laugh out loud. Brian was not jealous of his baby brother, as so often happens. He dearly loved his little brother and was mommy's helper. My brother, Mark, seemed to have a special connection with him. When Mark would come over to visit, he would usually just open the door and say, "Is anyone home?" Kyle's eyes would brighten, and he would get excited just at the sound of Mark's voice. He was such a loving little boy that my father called him "our Angel of Love."

The summer of 1972 was such a good summer. We went on camping trips and to a family reunion in Colorado. Kyle seemed to be doing very well, and our hearts were lightened with hopes and dreams for the future for both of our boys. In fact, we had always talked of adopting a child and we had started the process.

Then on September 26, 1972, Kyle seemed to be getting quite lethargic, worsening throughout the day. We were concerned, so that evening we met his doctor at the hospital once again. The decision was made to admit him and have a kidney specialist check on him in the morning. We were assured that he had beat so many odds in the past that the problem would be found and treated. We were told to go home and get a good night's sleep and not to worry. We again experienced that hesitant feeling of going to the elevator and leaving him there. All the doctor's assurances didn't really help much.

I remember so distinctly, however, the good night's sleep that we had. I believe that the Lord knew we would need it more than we ever had before. It was the next morning that our very worst nightmare came true when the telephone woke us from sleep. Our minds raced. We must wake Brian, dress him and take him with us. We needed to be together. We three needed each other now more than ever.

While in the car on the way to the hospital, we explained to Brian, "God has decided to take Kyle to heaven to live with him; and he won't be sick anymore."

After a period of silence, Brian suddenly asked, "Daddy and Mommy, there will be lots of food and toys in heaven for Kyle, won't there?" We assured him that God would take good care of Kyle. Out of the mouth of a four-year-old came the words of love and concern that warmed our hearts and briefly lightened the moment.

When we arrived at the hospital, Cy and I went directly to Kyle's room while a nurse looked after Brian. Kyle was still in his crib. I needed to touch him, but Cy just stood by the crib. I'm not sure how long we stayed there with our baby, whose skin was now cold and hard feeling; but reality could no longer be denied. We had lost our baby son who had been such a fighter, such a happy child, and who had brought us so much love. Our tears flowed; and reluctantly – very, very reluctantly – we left our eighteen-month-old precious child in that crib. His fight had ended, and he was at peace. However, peace seemed far away for us as we walked down the hall to a lounge to join Brian and some family and friends who were already gathering.

It was a struggle to leave the hospital. It seemed if we didn't leave maybe the situation would change; maybe it was all just a big mistake – maybe…But we finally did leave and go to a friend's home nearby. Several people gathered over the next few hours, including my parents who came from Wisconsin to be with us to lend their support and give us their love. Our shock was intensified because of all the other times Kyle had been hospitalized when we had great concern about if we would bring him home again; we did not even consider the possibility of losing him. But this time it was not to be. Instead of meeting with the specialist and hearing of treatment strategies for his recovery and making plans for another homecoming, and Kyle's future, we now were talking about a funeral. It was all too overwhelming – everything seemed to be a blur.

We were, of course, in shock! I have come to believe that shock is a great blessing to us at times of intense grief. It seems to put a person in an almost robotic state that allows one the strength to make the necessary plans for saying goodbye and for providing others an opportunity to do the same. The days often seem to run from one to another. Sleep is only the sporadic, exhausted, fitful kind; but by God's grace, we get through those times.

We had a memorial service at a funeral home in Minneapolis. Dear friends from our church, nurses from the hospital and many other people filled that room to capacity. Brian saw his brother and was allowed to touch him. Of course, we were concerned about how much a four-year-old could actually understand. But we knew it was important that he see our grief and understand that none of us would see Kyle again.

The funeral was held the next day in my home church in Luck, Wisconsin, where my parents and many relatives were members. A memorial flyer displayed Kyle's most recent picture. Even though it was taken just a few days before his death, he looked healthy. Our family cemetery plot is in Luck; and as we gathered around that small casket over the open grave, a friend of ours began leading the mourners in singing, "What a Friend We Have in Jesus." Leaving that graveside was next to impossible. My brother, Mark, gently led Cy and me back to our car. It was time to go back to the church – it was time to begin a whole new journey in our lives.

Kyle's journey on earth had ended. An eighteen-month struggle was over. Yet, during that time, much love, joy and real family bonding was experienced. We were focused on this child, determined to make his future as normal as possible. My father was a strong and thoughtful man; and during Kyle's struggle, he continued to describe him as, "An Angel of Love." Those words became the inscription alongside a lamb with a shepherd's staff on his gravestone.

We still had questions about what caused Kyle's death. The doctors explained that they hoped Kyle's case would further medical science if they could understand the source of the hemorrhage; so, we agreed to an autopsy. It was determined that an aneurysm had occurred at the base of his brain. An aneurysm is a weak spot in an artery that breaks. It had occurred during delivery and had gradually leaked blood until it caused symptoms that were manifested in seizures. It had healed itself. However, the body did not know when to halt the healing, and scar tissue eventually interfered with body functions such as respiratory. In 1972 little was known about the base of the brain, and performing surgery was never an option. So at the time, there was nothing that could have been done.

When Cy and I got married, we decided to have two homemade and two adopted children. Before Kyle died, we had already started the adoption process for a Korean daughter. Exactly nine months after Kyle's death, our miracle daughter, Kimberly Esther, arrived via Northwest Airlines. My parents and other close friends were at the airport for this very important delivery. What a joy!

Some may have thought that we were trying to replace Kyle. Let me assure you THAT WAS NOT THE CASE! I truly believe that you do not ever get over the death of a child. Nor should you expect to get over it. However, you do learn to live with the loss. Adding children to the family is not done to replace but rather to get on with life. We had given Kyle lots of love and attention, and now we needed to give that love to another child. Trying to focus on family again and giving special attention to the marriage are major factors in preserving the family unit.

Again in 1976 we adopted another child. Kevin, our Korean son, was 5 " years old when he joined our family. Both Kimberly and

Kevin have learned about Kyle and know that he was their brother too.

We were determined to keep Kyle's memory alive. While our children were growing up, we consistently took flowers and wreaths to the cemetery. Pictures of Kyle share our walls with pictures of Brian, Kevin and Kimberly. I wear a mother's ring with all four birthstones. When asked how many children we have, I often answer, "four." If questioned further, I'll say, "Three are living on earth and one is in heaven." Every parent, obviously, needs to answer such a question in the most comfortable way possible. Brian remembers his brother – especially making him laugh. When Kyle's birthday comes around, we talk about him and how old he would be. Sometimes tears are briefly shed; and always we wonder what he would look like now.

We have kept a small chest of drawers which stands in what we call Kyle's corner. A few special toys from Grandpa's and Grandma's, ceramic lambs, his baptism suit, his baby book, and scrapbooks of sympathy cards are stored in the drawers. Our other children's baby books are there too. On occasion we have given a special toy of Kyle's to a new baby. We once gave a nightlight of a praying child to a friend's new baby with the explanation that it had been Kyle's, which made it extra special to them. Speaking about Kyle Timothy is important to us because he was very much alive – a very real part of our lives; and we choose to share that with others.

We personally believe in heaven and eternity and lean on the hope of being reunited with Kyle one day. No, we won't get over his death; but by the grace of God, we have learned to live with the fact. We have found joy again in each other and in the three children that God has blessed us with here on earth. We have survived the death of our "Angel of Love;" and if such a tragedy should happen to you, we pray that you will find strength to begin life again and regain your hope for the future.

Reflections

Eighteen months seem rather brief in the normal span of a lifetime. However, that time impacted our lives in the most unforgettable ways possible! Many lessons were learned, particularly that of sensitivity when comforting and caring for grieving parents.

I was not aware that parents could request to hold a child that has just passed away. I regret deeply that I did not do that. It may not be important to every parent, but it would have helped me to accept Kyle's death. Some medical authorities will even have a stillborn baby cleaned up and dressed so that the parents can hold their child. It may be possible that mother's especially need this therapeutic time. Just touching and looking at the child is not the same as cuddling and holding the child until the parent feels that the time is right to let go. It's a time for parents to be alone with that child much as you may have been after the birth.

We became acutely aware that some people are very uncomfortable trying to console anyone who is grieving, but consoling parents is even more awkward. People desperately want to express their sympathy, but just do not know what to say or how to be helpful.

For instance, a friend tried to console me by saying, "Well, you are young, you can have other children."

I wanted to scream at her, "I don't want another child, I want this one!"

A dear person patted me on the shoulder and said, "You are strong, you'll get through this."

"I don't feel strong; please let me be weak," I wanted to cry.

Someone else gave me a hug, which felt so good, and then followed it with these two words, "I understand." The hug lost its warmth because she hadn't lost a child, and there was no way that she could possibly understand.

We also heard, "It's God's will." Whatever a person's religious convictions, this isn't the time to hear that God's will is to take children away from their loving families. Even to presume that you would know God's will can be offensive.

"God just needed another little angel," we were told.

The above comments were not helpful and were often hurtful even though they were said by people who loved us. So what's a person to say and do at such a time?

Your presence is absolutely invaluable. JUST BE THERE, hug, cry and say, "I'm so sorry."

"You are all in our prayers" is a valued assurance. Or, just be honest, "I just don't know what to say; I can't imagine how devastating this is; just know that we love you." Then see if there's anything you can do from washing dishes to running errands. JUST BE THERE and be available. Remember that hugs and tears say more to the grieving than any so-called words of wisdom ever could.

A comforting thing to do is to recall some endearing qualities of the deceased, especially for a child. Remembering how cute, loving, a wonderful smile, or any other special memory can be so special to recall. It's important to talk about the child with the parents after the funeral is over when it can seem as though every one else has already forgotten. This keeps the child alive in our memories.

The loss of a child is a completely life-changing event. When a child dies, a part of the parent dies too. It feels as though a part of your very being is ripped away; a part of your own life dies. All deaths are traumatic. All deaths have their own devastating effects, but the death of a child is really different. The future changes when a child is born; plans are made, and the parents expect to live on in their children. When that child dies, the future changes again. Children aren't supposed to die before their parents. They are to live on and carry on the legacy of the family they are born or adopted into. We look at our children, and we see a future that will continue even after we die. When our child dies, that future also dies.

It's not just the future that changes, the present also changes most dramatically. All our love and energies (in the case of a long-term illness) has been put into caring for that child. When a sudden death occurs, the shock can be so overwhelming that a deep sense of hopelessness may overtake the family.

Experiencing a real sense of guilt can be quite normal. Even though everything possible had been done, many nagging questions can raise their ugly heads. How could we have done something more or differently? Should we have obtained even another medical opinion? If only we hadn't left the hospital. If only we hadn't chosen that course of action. I also questioned whether I had taken proper care of myself during my pregnancy. If only, if only, if only... These thoughts can haunt you over and over and become like an infection that eats away at the mind and eventually the body. It's so important to deal with the "if only's" before they rip away at the very fabric of the family.

Believe it or not at a time when family members need each other the most, when an intact and supportive family is so important, many families break apart. The divorce rate after the death of a child is quite high. The other children in the family need the love and support of their parents. They need to know that they aren't going to die tomorrow just because their brother or sister did. They need to know that it was through no fault of theirs that this tragedy happened. They need to remake their lives; but they also need to have a time of grief that is very personal to each one of them individually. Parents who are in the deepest tomb of grief possible still need to be there to meet the needs of their grieving children. It's overwhelming; and sadly for many couples, it seems totally impossible.

So how is it possible to stay together, to actually meet this challenge and come out of this experience an intact, family unit? I can only speak from our experience. We were blessed with very caring and supportive families and friends – people who kept in touch and continued to grieve with us. I believe that our marriage vows and commitment became more meaningful to us and were actually the cement that held us together. That doesn't mean that recovery wasn't tough; IT WAS! I truly believe that men and women often grieve quite differently – at least we did. I cry easily and Cy doesn't; sometimes my abundant tears became a source of irritation. Cy needs to be busy and allowed to be angry. That's OK! Because people are still most likely living in a blur, it is easy to judge how each other handles their own personal grief. I believe the fact that the woman has carried that child for nine months gives her the feeling that she has known that child longer than the father has. At times when we should have been experiencing warmth and support from one another, we chose to exclude the other and deal with our feelings alone. Upon reflection, even though at the time it felt like alienation, it may have been necessary for individual recovery. Our love for each other would not allow the chasm to get so wide that it could not be closed.

Out of necessity, Cy was forced to return to work after just a few days. Although it was difficult and the great loss of Kyle was always in his mind, he was forced to concentrate on his job during the day. When he came home in the evening, however, he was greeted at the door again with our sad reality. I was an at-home-mom, and the concentrated efforts that Kyle's care had required had now come to an abrupt end. I was back caring for just one child. The house seemed as empty as I felt! Even though we had much outside support, I still felt completely alone; and although I knew deep in my heart that it was not true, I still felt completely unneeded. As you know, the worst ache in the world is heartache. One day all I wanted to do was to make it stop. I found myself in the bathroom with a handful of Excedrin just below my mouth. I stood there for quite some time thinking that I really could make the hurt and the ache go away. I don't know why I didn't take them; I'm just thankful that I didn't. I am sure that God spoke to me in some way, and my heart heard His words.

It takes a long time for life to get back to normal. When it does, normal takes on a new meaning. With God's help the adjustments are made; and even though we never forget the child we once held in our arms, we do learn to live our lives with the loss.

dw

God's Boy

Several weeks had passed since the death of our precious Kyle. Understandably, Brian was feeling the separation and grief along with Cy and me. His four-year-old mind was trying hard to make sense of his loss.

One day he asked me, "Mommy, am I your boy?"

I took him in my arms and assured him that he certainly was our very precious boy.

"Well, then," he replied, "You have one boy now, and God has one boy too."

dw

Brian and Kyle in Matching Outfits.

He Lived Boldly in God's Grace

It was April 1974 and I was becoming paranoid about early morning hours. Why was it that bad news often seemed to come between midnight and 6 A.M.? When the telephone rang, it was panic time! I knew I must answer it, but I preferred not for fear of an unwelcome life-changing message.

This 6 A.M. call was no different. It was a call that was about to change the rest of my life along with the lives of many people I love. The person responding to my "hello" was my dad. "Are you sitting down, Kay?" he asked in a strained and broken voice. Struggling, he cried out two more words, "Mark's dead!"

"Mark's what?" my body shrieked.

"It was a single car accident. He hit the bridge on the road by the Price place. We've lost him!"

That was it for now; the explanations would come later. Just the hard, cold fact was in those two words. My brother was alive when I went to bed, and now I woke up and learned that he was gone.

"We'll be on our way home as soon as possible," I assured Dad. It seemed as though I had just been plunged into a thick fog.

My body heaved with tears as I tried to explain to Cy what my dad had just told me. He called his work, and we proceeded to grab some things and prepare our five year old Brian and baby Kimberly for the trip. Once again we began that early morning drive to my childhood farm in Wisconsin.

My heart was asking, "How could this be happening again?" It was just eighteen months earlier that we had buried our eighteen-month-old son, Kyle. Mark seemed to have a special connection with him. When Mark would come into our home he would usually yell, "Is anyone home?" as he was opening the door. The minute Kyle heard his voice he would kick and get wide-eyed and excited even before he saw him. Kyle needed physical therapy because of some motor problems, and Mark would get down on the floor and work with him like none of the rest of us ever could. Kyle would beam at Mark and let him exercise his legs and arms. Later as we stood at Kyle's grave, after the others had gone back to the church, it was Mark who took me by the arm with tenderness and love and pried me away from the graveside. It was just a year and a half later; and now my twenty-eight-year-old brother, just three years younger than me, was gone.

On the way out of the city, we stopped at the job site where Mark had been working and gave the supervisor the bad news. Mark had become an ironworker (the same trade as Cy is in) building office buildings and other large structures. He was a big man who always liked to live on the edge. It seemed that Mark was always looking for new physical challenges. He drove about an hour and forty-five minutes to work every day. Just as with Cy, being an ironworker seemed to fit him, at least for that time in his life.

My thoughts wandered to Mark's six-year-old son, Randy, who was now fatherless. Then I thought of his wife, Cheryl; I couldn't even fathom the devastation of being 29 and a widow. "It's too much, Lord; IT'S JUST TOO MUCH!"

After a couple of hours, the mailbox was in sight; and we turned into the long driveway leading the way up the hill to the farm. It looked the same: a red barn, chicken coop, granary, woodshed and the two-story white farmhouse. I had a good up-bringing here by God-fearing parents. I always liked coming back for visits. We stopped the car and Randy ran out to meet us. We were hardly out of the car when we heard him saying, "Don't be too sad, Aunt Kay and Uncle Cy, because now my daddy can take care of baby Kyle in heaven." WOW! I was without words and just hugged him.

Mom and Dad were in the kitchen with Cheryl and my brother, Dale. We all hugged and cried; and, once again, I knew with great intensity how important family is. We loved each other so much and that's the way it should be. But oh, how it hurts when one of these family members is taken away. It is said that the more you love, the more it hurts when you are separated. The pain can't be explained; it can only be experienced.

"How did it happen?" we asked. We were told that Mark had gone to run a late errand in preparation for his in-laws coming for a weekend visit. Cheryl and Randy had gone to sleep. She awoke in the early morning and realized Mark wasn't beside her. She panicked and called my parents, my brother Dale, and some friends who came over to their home right away. They started driving the country roads. Less than one mile from Mark and Cheryl's home Dale and Dad found him. His MG car had hit a bridge and overturned on him. Dad knew immediately that he had just found his son – dead. Of course, Dale also realized that his brother was gone. I can't even begin to imagine the terror that must rip through a person's whole being to find a loved one like that. Now, they not only had to notify the authorities, but they also had to tell Mark's wife and son, Mom and sister. That job fell on my dad's shoulders.

Of those in the kitchen that morning, Mom seemed to be the most inconsolable. I understood that more than anyone else. I, too, had lost a son. I, too, had to say goodbye to a child that I had carried for nine months in my womb and then labored to give birth to. I don't remember talking about it, but we now had something very intense in common. We had both lost sons. Mark had supported me just 18 months earlier when my son died. Then suddenly Mom and Dad's son and my brother was in heaven with my son. What a path we were on! Many had trod it before; it was well worn; but when we found ourselves there, it seemed as though we were the first. Death is so personal that whenever we lose someone we love, it seems as though we are the only ones who have ever had this experience. As Mom sat by the table with her head in her hands weeping, Dad walked around behind her and gently put his big, rough farmer's hands on her shoulders. With tears streaming down his cheeks, he said, "Esther, the sun will shine again."

"The sun will shine again," my dad had told my mom. My dad's quiet faith had shown brightly as he comforted my mother. His statement was unforgettable for me. The cloud of grief in the house at that point was gray and heavy. The tears fell like rain. Just a few hours earlier Dad had been the one to find his first born son the victim of a deadly car crash; now here he was holding His Heavenly Father's hand and receiving all the strength he needed to give the rest of us assurance and hope.

We were glad that Cheryl's parents and her sister and family already had plans for coming to visit that weekend. She needed them, and they would be there that afternoon.

When I reflect on traumatic times, it always amazes me how we get the strength to do what needs to be done. I view 'shock' as a gift that somehow insulates us just enough to get through those tough days before and after the funeral. In that extreme stress, we seem to operate on almost no sleep and yet get through each hour and each day. God gives us the gift of shock – later he gives us the strength we need when reality truly hits. He walks with us then as He walks with us in the good times. In fact, I think it would be more accurate to say that He carries us then.

The funeral was in the larger church in the town of Luck because our country church was too small. The church was packed. He had known so many people in his short life. He too was buried in the family cemetery where Kyle was buried. Not long afterwards, Cheryl put up a big gravestone that reads "He Lived Boldly in God's Grace." That explains Mark's life! There certainly are no answers for such a tragic early death other than it's just the kind of world we live in. Tragedy can happen to any one, at any time.

We are all someone's child. Usually we expect that when we are in our fifties or sixties or even older, we will lose our parents. Losing a child is the wrong order – it just shouldn't be that way. We expect to be at least middle-aged before we say goodbye to our siblings. It didn't work that way for Dale and me. There is eleven years between us in age. Dale was just 20 years old when his big brother died.

Sympathy for the parents, wife and children is overwhelming, as it should be. I think that brothers and sisters are sometimes a bit overlooked. I now try very hard to remember the whole family when there is a death. I don't assume that they know I am thinking about them, I make sure they know.

I am eleven years older than Dale, and I really missed out on his growing up years. Mark had three more years at home with him. I was told that one day Dale asked, "Dad, will I ever get as tall as Mark?" Dale had been ten years old when Mark graduated from high school and then moved to Minneapolis for a while – but they had several years together at home.

After meeting Cy, Mark decided to go to work as an ironworker. He married Cheryl and they lived in Minneapolis for a while, but the country had Mark's heart. They eventually purchased some land and a nice mobile home and moved within a few miles of our parents. Dale then got to see Mark a lot more often. Even though Mark was eight years older, when Dale started school, their relationship grew as brothers.

Dale was strong during the days before the funeral when visitors came and went and preparations were made for our final goodbye. Mom became concerned for him as weeks passed because she felt that he wasn't allowing himself to grieve, and he was withdrawing. Maybe he was like many men who think men don't cry; I am not sure. I know that we are all on our own grief timetable. Yet, maybe he felt he needed to stay strong for our parents so he stuffed his own feelings. Finally one day my mother called to tell me that Dale had broken down and released his anger and sadness.

I felt somewhat lost too. After all, I was Mark's sister. We had been only three years apart. We had gone to school together, played together and worked together as we were growing up. We had double dated when going with the people we eventually married. Cy and I were married six weeks after Mark's and Cheryl's wedding. He had been such a help when we had our *Angel of Love*. He grieved deeply when Kyle died. When Mark died I felt that some of my source of strength was gone; and no one really understood. I may just have been feeling sorry for myself, but feelings are real. The good news was that I was Mark's sister – the other good news is that I always will be.

Another life had been snuffed out so quickly. Once again our faith was tested. Recovery takes time because grief is not on a schedule. Even in our darkest hours God was there for us. I am sure that He cried with us and carried us through yet another path in this "Deep Woods."

In June of 1992, I wrote my brother a letter which I'm sharing with you here.

Dear Mark,

It sure is a long time since we've talked, or argued, or teased, or hugged for that matter. I've thought a lot about you during your eighteen-year absence. We were quite a team during our growing up years.

You certainly were a rascal. You often nearly gave Mom and Dad heart attacks. Since you were three years younger than I, I thought I was in control – that is, until one day when we were scuffling around in the kitchen. Somehow, you got ahold of my one leg and my one arm and started twirling me around the kitchen. You thought that it was extremely funny, and I was horrified at the thought that you were now stronger than I was. I guess it was your turn.

You started your shenanigans at a rather young age. The summer when you were three years old, Dad and some neighbors were shingling the barn. Mom had prepared lunch and asked you to go and tell Daddy that it was ready. There was a ladder and scaffolding on the East Side of the barn, but the men had gone over the peak to the west side to work. So, of course, in your three-year-old mind it made perfect sense to crawl up the ladder and peek over the top of the roof and say, "Daddy, it's lunch time." Needless to say, the men were shocked and frightened for you. Dad obviously reached for you and helped you down. We had a picture of you at the peak of that roof. No one would have believed it otherwise.

Like most brothers and sister, we surely could fight;, but we played together a lot too. Hey, do you remember how we played in that big tree that blew down in the pasture? We made little rooms among the branches. Then one day we got really sophisticated and built a tree house below the hill from the house. Dad gave us scrap lumber to use and all the nails we needed. We made it a two-story work of art. I don't remember that we argued; we really worked together on that project.

You were always the one getting into mischief, right? Right!! You were so daring; like pumping so high on the swing that the rope would double up. One time it broke and you landed in the hospital with a concussion.

Remember how we grew beans for the factory in Frederic? When we got old enough we had our own patches. If we took care of them, we made the money. We absolutely hated it when we had to go up north and pick blueberries with Mom and sometimes aunts and cousins.

I think of you now, and I smile. You were like a cat with nine lives. If only you wouldn't have tried for a tenth. You fell out of haymows; drove the homemade jeep through frozen ice; rolled your motor scooter; tried going down the water slide at the high school standing on your feet – just to name a few incidents and accidents. You would often get hurt to some extent and then try again.

I hope that you are not getting tired of my story telling, but I've got one more. You were pretty little this time too. Chores were being done so Dad was in the barn, and I was a silent witness. You stepped up behind a cow and boldly pulled her tail. She, of course, reacted with a kick that shoved you into the wall. Well, she only made you mad! You didn't cry; you just got up and went for her tail again.

Lucky for you, dad snatched you up before you had another chance at tail pulling.

For three years you walked with me to and from Lincoln School which was a mile and a half away. In the winter we would take our sled and race down Riley's Hill. Then we took the bus together to North Star School for two years before getting transferred to Frederic Schools.

You were eight and I was eleven when Mom and Dad told us that we were going to have a new brother or sister. Dale was born, and we had another brother. He is very different from you in many ways, Mark.

I wasn't around for your high school years except when you were a freshman. That was the same year that Dale was in first grade. I would love to have been there for your prom dates and football games. They had to order special sized football shoes for you; you grew to be a big man.

Remember where you went after you graduated from high school? Yep, down to sister Kay's in Minneapolis. I became the one you hit up for a little extra spending money. I was also the one to buy you a Volkswagen that you quickly demolished. Mark, you didn't wait around for life to find you; you went out and found it!

I wasn't done with you though. I had started working at the headquarters of The American Lutheran Church, and I spotted a girl I thought that you should meet and even date. Lo and behold! You agreed with me. After a lot of typical Mark persistence, she agreed too. As we all know, the result was "I do's" and your son, Randy. Hey, kid, remember those double dates with Cy and me? It was almost scary how much alike you and Cy were.

Snowmobiles! We all had snowmobiles including Dale. Weekends we often spent on the farm snowmobiling together. It was a chance for us women to try to get as good as you men. We jumped snow banks and raced probably just about as good as you did. Those are days that are forever etched in my memory.

You had a lot going for you, Mark. I surely wonder how different things would have been if you hadn't let your car get the best of you.

I'm almost fifty now. Cy and I just celebrated our 25th Wedding Anniversary. You made a good Groomsman that day. I'll never forget how supportive and caring you were during our Kyle's crisis. He would let you help him with physical therapy like no one else could. He also knew who was there when you would open our door and shout, "Anyone home?"

I've gained a few pounds and raised three kids. Brian is almost twenty-four, and in many ways, a lot like you. He is daring and likes milking every ounce out of life. He's traveled from coast to coast and has now settled on being an ironworker. He also has a very big heart – just like you.

Your precious little Kimberly is a beautiful young lady now. You loved her so much the few months that you knew her. I have the picture of you two on her Baptism Day on my wall. Now she is struggling with college and decisions for her future. She's got a good head. She'll do just fine.

I don't know how much you know, because I've never been where you are. But I think that you were probably watching over Kevin Mark during the war in the gulf last year. He's our handsome Korean son who's been with us for sixteen years. Yes, he's named after you. He is married to a beautiful girl named, Brenda. Kevin is a Lance Corporal in Intelligence in the Marine Corp. You would be proud of him too!

Your son, Randy, is in Texas. We don't hear from him, but we do hear from his mother that he is happy and successful in his job as a sales representative. He is almost twenty-five; it's hard to believe, isn't it? He is handsome like you were, Mark.

Your wife, Cheryl, has made a new life for herself. I'm sure that's the way you would have wanted it.

Our brother, Dale, is married to Debbie. They met in Eau Claire when Dale was going to school. They have a son, Soren, and two daughters, Leah and Elizabeth. Dale missed you desperately after you left. He counted on his big brother for a lot of things. You will be happy to know that he is an architect and doing just fine.

You are probably wondering when these ramblings will end. I wonder what life would have been like if you were still around. Cy is still an ironworker. Would you still have been one too? Well, knucklehead, you didn't have to leave this planet so young you know!

Cy and I are looking at retirement in a few years. Hey, quit laughing you would probably have a few gray hairs by now too! After living in Minneapolis for thirty-one years, we are preparing to move back to Wisconsin. We are on a five-year- do-it-yourself plan, with 11 acres of woods just east of Hudson. We love it here!

You have a lot of company now. Dale and I are the only two left here. I trust that you will cuddle Kyle for me, give both Mom and Dad hugs, and greet sister-in-law, Carlene, and Cy's folks too. I love you! See you someday!

Missing you,
Sis Kay

P.S. Mark, it's me again. It's now 2003. We are now grandparents to Kevin and Brenda's year old little Taylor Joy. Oh, what a true "joy" and gift she is. We have been in our dream home in the woods for 5 years and love it. Brian and Cy own Erectors Inc. Kimberly is a Legal Secretary. Kevin works in the financial world, and Brenda is an executive in the retail world. I am now sixty and Cy is right behind me. Oh yes, we saw Randy a couple of years ago and spent a lot of time visiting about you. Leah has been with you for over a year now, and she is so missed by all of us. Soren and Elizabeth are young adults pursuing their futures. Dale is about a year away from fifty and has excelled in his career as an architect. Debbie still loves teaching children. No matter how much time goes by, my dear brother, you are still missed.

dw

Kay Marie and Mark

A Journey Some Must Take

Life After the Death of a Child

When I think of the word journey I usually think of a trip or an adventure. I usually anticipate fun, excitement and creating wonderful memories. However, I always know that my adventure will end and life will return to its familiar routines.

There are certain journeys that last a lifetime. Some are chosen and enhance our lives. Some, we would never choose. One such journey is that of reconstructing our life after the death of a child. This journey lasts for a lifetime.

Within 18 months, my mother and father, and my husband and I buried sons. One was a small child – one was an adult; both were beloved children. Though we didn't speak of it much as a common journey, we knew we were all four walking it together.

Twenty-seven years passed, and Mom and Dad joined their son and their grandson in heaven. My brother, Dale, and I are now the only ones left in the family of our birth. My husband and I have three grown children living on earth and one in heaven, and Dale and Debbie had three children born to them. That was about to change.

One day in early October 2001, after a year-long struggle with brain cancer, Dale and Debbie's 19 year-old daughter Leah's life on earth ended. Now, they are on their own journey that parents who have lost children must take. We have the same journey in common. Oh yes, we are at very different places on that road; but we are on it together. Isn't it ironic that from our small family our parents and their two remaining children have taken the same journey?

The road is crowded, and at times very lonely. The journey lasts a lifetime, and can be extremely rough. I do not know how that journey can be walked and how one can again become whole without holding our Heavenly Father's hand. The year after the death is packed full of "firsts": first birthday, first Christmas, first vacation trip, first everything without that child. It's like having our heart ripped from our chest and then having it broken over and over again. Eventually, by the grace of God, time softens these events a little; and we are given the strength to keep walking "the road.

When I hear of the death of a child, I immediately pray for the family, especially the parents. Almost every time that we hear the daily news or read the paper there is another story and another grieving family with parents who are beginning the journey.

Almost 30 years after Kyle died, our pastor during the Easter Sunday Worship Service included a prayer for those who had lost children. I instinctively gasped! My friend put her hand over mine, and the tears silently rolled down my cheeks. Later she turned to me and commented, "It never goes away, does it?" I replied, "No it doesn't, and I wouldn't want it to."

This I know for sure: The only way I could have walked this road, with the grief that trips us up; with the darkness that at times surrounds us like a tomb; with the questions that want to be answered and may never be in this life; and with the hole that is left and will never be filled, is knowing that God understands.

I know that God understands because He also saw his child, Jesus, die. I know that with His love and His hand leading me on this road, I will take this journey with my brother and all the others on the road day-by-day. By God's grace He gives us the strength to live with our loss and to complete our journey on this earth until we are united with the children we lost for only a time.

dw

We'll Celebrate Later

Christmas had come and gone. It had been different – very different that year. For the first time in my life, we had not celebrated this special time with my parents.

In early November my mother and father had traveled to Hot Springs, Arkansas to get help for my mother's severe arthritis at a Medical Health Center and Spa equipped with all the latest gadgets and specialists in the area. There was a medical doctor and several physical therapists to guide her treatment. She had started having severe symptoms about six weeks after my brother Mark had died. The doctors called it stress-onset arthritis. As the weather was getting colder in Wisconsin, they were enjoying the milder temperatures of Arkansas. They had rented a tiny apartment near the Health Center, and Dad could push Mom in her wheelchair to the Center for her therapeutic treatments. He could also walk downtown to the grocery store and the drug store if he wished.

They soon met other retired couples and made some friends, especially one couple whose names were Jack and Sylvia. My father had worked physically hard all of his life, and now he had the opportunity to sit outside and visit with other fellows about the same age as he was. It was like a vacation for him with someone else to care for Mom for a while during the day.

The therapy was painful for Mom, especially in the beginning; but they both agreed that it was worth a try. Mom was tough and hung in with the treatments; consequently, after a few weeks they were able to see some real improvement and were feeling that it was indeed good they had come to the Center. Then just a few days before Christmas Daddy called and said that they felt they should stay awhile longer because Mom was at a point where maybe a couple more weeks could make a big difference in the long-term. That meant, of course, that they wouldn't be home for Christmas. So we decided we would get together as soon as possible after they returned to celebrate a late Holiday.

Then Dad added, "Maybe your Mom and I will even be able to make that trip to Alaska to see my sister Helen and her family." He had always yearned for and dreamed about making that trip. His voice was really excited and filled with hope as he shared with me. A few days later we celebrated Christmas with a phone call and a promise of, "We'll see you soon."

New Years 1983 came, and we made our plans and resolutions as we did every year. After all, there was a whole year ahead for accomplishing many things we had always planned on doing. It was especially exciting to think about the trip that Mom and Dad were hoping to make to Anchorage. Then in an instant, life took another turn.

The telephone was ringing, I forced my eyes to look at the clock – it was only 2 A.M. My throat tightened as I lifted the receiver and hesitantly said, "Hello."

I heard my Mother's voice. She was matter of fact and said, "Now be strong Kay." I had heard those words before, and I detested them. "Your Dad just died," she continued. No trying to soften the message or beat around the bush. Just the hard news – that's all. I don't even recall my words. I do know that I asked, "Mom, where are you?"

"I am in the apartment."

"Are you alone?" "What happened?" " Where is Dad?" the questions poured out.

Then it dawned on me that my crippled Mother was in Arkansas in a relatively strange city. There would be things that would need to be done. In her physical condition she certainly couldn't handle things alone.

"Mom" I said, "I will call you back as soon as I get airline reservations and call Dale."

I had been in this place before. I was not a stranger to the "Deep Woods" of grief but – but, this was my dad. In a daze I told Cy; I shifted to automatic pilot and found an airline that would give me a last minute grief-ticket on a flight that left at 6 A.M. I called Dale, who lived in Eastern Wisconsin with his wife and children. I woke him from his night's sleep, and I gave him the devastating news. He was only 29 years old, which is way too young to lose his father. He was just starting a family of his own and his children needed their grandfather.

I quickly threw some clothes in a suitcase. We waited until the very last minute to gently wake our children and bring them downstairs to the Living Room where we asked them to sit together on the sofa. Our children had experienced death as recently as one month earlier when we had all said, "goodbye" to their Aunt Carlene who had died very young from colon cancer.

We proceeded to tell them that their Grandfather had joined Brother Kyle, Uncle Mark and Aunt Carlene in heaven. They were still sleepy and probably didn't fully comprehend what we were telling them, but they did understand that I had to go and get Grandma. They were concerned that I would need some money if I had to go on an airplane, so they all trotted up to their rooms and scrounged around gathering their few dollars and cents together to give me for my trip.

I got on the plane at a little after 6 A.M. I was so thankful that I was assigned a window seat. I remember looking out at the clouds. It was then that I was really struck with the reason why I was there. The tears streamed down my face, and I felt like I was searching for my daddy somewhere above the clouds. It just seemed that I should be able to see him up there somewhere on his way to heaven. Maybe I could see him just one more time – maybe we could even wave to each other.

Daddy had been Mom's caretaker, and he was considered the healthy one. Who would ever have believed that he would leave this world before Mom? Even though the plane was filled, I felt isolated and alone. I could pray for strength now and for God's hand to take mine through the next days. I had to change planes in Memphis to make a connection to Little Rock. I was so glad to have those hours behind me when we landed.

My folk's friends, Jack and Sylvia, were at the airport, just as Mom had said that they would be when I had called her back and told her of my flight schedule. As I sat in the back seat of their car, I pumped them for the details of what had happened.

It seemed like a very long ride. Finally, I was in my mother's arms; and we were holding each other very tightly. It was only ten hours since she had called us, and I was still trying to get it through my head that Dad would not be walking through the door to give me a hug.

We sat down and Mom explained that they had gone to bed. A while later Dad had awakened with what he thought was a stomachache. He crawled out of bed to go to the bathroom and collapsed on the floor at the foot of the bed. I'm not sure which came first. I do know that she knocked on the wall with her cane for help. I believe she was the one to call 911, and somehow Jack and Sylvia heard the commotion too. Anyway, before long the paramedics came. My dad never did regain consciousness. Jack and Sylvia actually went to the emergency room while Mom stayed at the apartment. She felt that it would just have taken too long for her to get ready and loaded in the car. She wanted someone to go right then. It probably seemed like an eternity for my Mother, wondering what Dad's condition was. However, I guess it wasn't really very long before Jack and Sylvia came back. They gave the news to my Mother that Daddy had actually died before the paramedics arrived. She was assured that he had suffered very little because he had a massive heart attack. For a while we could hardly think; we just sat together. Soon she insisted that I go to the tiny kitchen and make us a lunch. My Danish Mother was concerned that I eat.

The hospital had put Dad's body in custody of a local funeral home. They wanted me to go there to make arrangements for getting him back to Luck, Wisconsin. I wasn't feeling very confident about the whole process. I wanted to be sure we wouldn't be taken advantage of. So, I called the funeral home in Luck. We knew the owners well. They had handled my Grandparents arrangements as well as those for Mark and Kyle. It was good to talk to them and to find out exactly what the procedure for transportation should be including some price guideline to use. One of the workers at the Health Center had offered to give me a ride so I called her, and she picked me up. Once again Mom chose to stay at her apartment.

I found myself in a very strange and surreal situation. Suddenly, we were talking about finding cargo space on a plane for my father. Not first class or coach, but room in the cargo space. My head knew that was the way it had to be done; but my heart was broken, and I couldn't accept that we were doing the right thing. The plane he would arrive in at the Minneapolis/St. Paul International Airport would be different than the one we were taking. Someone from the Funeral Home in Luck would be there to meet the plane. I was thankful that the price was within the guidelines I was given.

The Funeral Director that I worked with was very compassionate. He even offered to take me back to Mom's apartment and to stop along the way at a Drug Store to get a prescription for her. I was so grateful for his thoughtfulness, patience and help.

A little more that twelve hours after I had received the call from my Mother, I had flown across country and had made arrangements to fly my deceased father home. Next, we had to make return reservations for Mom and me for the day after next. I set about looking for the tickets. Mom said that Dad had hidden them in the top dresser drawer. I looked and looked but they weren't there. I found Dad's wallet, but no tickets. I decided to give up for a while and started packing his and Mom's suitcases. I tenderly folded and packed Dad's clothing and hesitantly closed his suitcase. Once again I looked all over the apartment and could not find the airline tickets; again I gave up. I called the Health Center to make arrangements to talk to the person in charge of Mom's care. Since she was quitting her therapy early, I wanted to know if there was anything that we could do to continue the program that was started. What medications, food supplements, exercises etc. was she on? We would go there the next morning.

When we arrived back at Mom's apartment, I resumed my search for the airline tickets without success. We prayed. I went to that top dresser drawer one more time. I picked up the newspaper that was used as a liner and there they were – under the liner of the drawer. My dad had truly hidden them so they would not get lost. We both were so relieved. Since they were open-ended tickets, we knew that at least

Mom could use hers. I called the airline and was given permission to fly home on my dad's ticket. What a blessing! There was a shuttle from Hot Springs to the airport in Little Rock that we made arrangements to take.

The pastor of Mom and Dad's church needed to be called so a funeral date could be set. The service and the lunch afterwards needed to be discussed. Some things could be left until we got back to Luck, but I made another call to my brother for his input regarding the arrangements. I called Mom's sister, my Aunt Myrtle, to update her and checked in with my family. God was giving me strength and a calm spirit to handle all these things long distance.

It had been a busy day. Tomorrow we would need to clean the apartment so it could be rented again, finish packing, and go to the Health Center. We went to bed early because we were both exhausted. I was so glad that Mom was able to sleep. However, I laid awake most of that night on the side of the bed that my dad had slept on just the night before. I was probably just too exhausted and had too much on my mind to sleep.

The next morning I made us breakfast and helped my mother get dressed. We got her situated in the wheelchair and then to the appointment at the Health Center. They gave me a tour and I spoke with the professionals who were in charge of her treatment. I was very impressed with everyone and everything that I saw. They all talked about Daddy and expressed their sympathy offering any help they could give. In the midst of our grief, several gracious helpers had come forth. They were like beacons of light breaking through the darkness.

We went back to the apartment to finish packing and clean up the apartment so Mom could move out. One more day had passed.

We had an early shuttle to catch the next morning and a plane to board in Little Rock for Minneapolis with a stop over in Memphis. When I presented my ticket at the counter, I explained our situation and that I had been told I could use Dad's ticket. She confirmed that; and told us that if we had any trouble in Memphis, we were to have them call her. Back then, that kind of communication was possible.

We had about three hours in Memphis. Mom, of course, needed a wheelchair. I had a couple of carry-on pieces of luggage plus our purses balanced on Mom's lap and hanging from the handles of the wheelchair. We found a nice restaurant, and we both were ready for a decent meal. When we were starting for the gate, I decided that we needed to get a SkyCap to help us to our departure gate.

God sent us a very beautiful man. He was an older man who seemed to intuitively know we were not on vacation. Before we knew it Mom was telling him everything. She cried a little, and he listened and tenderly gave his condolences. He was like a breath of fresh air for us. When we reached the gate, we proceeded to hand him a tip. He refused it, saying, " Someday, someone will help me out when I need it; please let me do this for you." We thanked him and bid him, "goodbye." He had been a very bright spot in an otherwise rather dark afternoon for us.

It was an uneventful flight, and Cy and the kids were at the airport to meet us at about 7 PM. I was really getting anxious to be home because I knew that clothes would have to be washed, and we would have to pack for our family of five for several days and be ready to leave for Luck by noon the next day. The Funeral Home wanted us to come in as soon as we could that afternoon with Dad's clothes and to finish all the details waiting for us.

When we got to our home, we were pleased that the pastor from our church in Minneapolis came to visit us even though there was much to do. He knew my parents, and it was so good to have him there with us for awhile.

The next couple of days are now somewhat a blur. My brother and his family had arrived; my cousin from Alaska came; and the evening of the visitation at the funeral home was upon us. As I was standing at the casket with my family, looking at my daddy, I suddenly became very weak in my knees; and Cy had to catch me. He led me to a seat where I stayed the rest of the evening. My exhaustion had caught up with me.

The funeral was the next day. Once again we found ourselves at the cemetery where there was a gravestone for "Our Angel of Love" and for Brother Mark who had lived boldly in God's Grace. We drove the car very close so Mom could just open the door and hear everything. She was laying to rest her husband of over forty years.

We spent time after the funeral luncheon at my cousin's place looking through cards and memorials together with my brother and his wife. We were already thinking of needing to go back to our respective homes.

Memorials, in memory of – memories. We all have our memories. I have a very special one. My dad always gave me a gift when we got together. His gift to me was a foot massage. He had purchased a book about foot reflexology and had studied it. He knew just where to massage to relieve what ailed me. It always felt sooo good. Some months before they left for Arkansas they had come to our home for the weekend. We were sitting in our den. Mom was in her favorite chair and I was sitting with my foot on Dad's knee as he was working his magic on my feet. At that moment the thought that crossed my mind was, " I can't imagine ever being without these two special people." I truly could not imagine it so I pushed the thought out of my mind. I have thought of that afternoon many times since, and the warmth of that moment brings me comfort.

Dad was the quiet one – the oh so honest one. His example spoke loudly to his family and to his many friends. His faith was strong. He recounted an Angel coming to him one day in this way.

Dad's father was in Idaho for a few years staying with Dad's twin brothers. One noon after eating he went to his corner chair to relax and nap a bit. He had been a little perplexed because he couldn't quit thinking about his father and even seemed to be a bit worried about him. After sitting a bit, he said that he suddenly saw a shadowy figure of a woman in a long white dress in front of him. She told him her name and said, "Do not worry, your father is just fine." She then disappeared and a deep peace descended upon him.

My father is now at peace again – at peace with his Heavenly Father and maybe even in the presence of the Angel that came to him that day when he needed her.

dw

Her Bags Were Packed

She sat in a big easy chair that moved up and down at the touch of a button, in a corner, in a room that was her home, in a building that housed a hundred other old people. She needed help to dress, to be seated into her wheelchair, to go to the dining room, to get into and out of bed, and for all of her personal needs. Pain, sometimes intense, was her constant companion. One of her good days would probably be almost unbearable for most people. A body that was once straight and proud was consistently shrinking. Her long, slender neck was gone, and her head was resting on her shoulders. Hands that once milked cows, prepared corn for canning, scrubbed other people's homes for added income, and dried her children's tears had become crippled and almost useless. Her fingers struggled to hold a pen to write her name, grasp a spoon, or lift a small glass. Long scars decorated both knees where artificial ones replaced those given to her at birth. She was my mother.

Mom's mind was still clear and sharp, but her body was much older than her last birthday said it should be. People came to her because she was a very good listener, and they treasured her advice and wisdom. I knew she still had some spunk when she would chide me for not calling her on the phone more often. Since my dad died, her husband of forty-two years, loneliness became almost overwhelming at times. Her hands became unable to hold books making it impossible for her to enjoy her favorite pastime. A few selected television programs and her many memories filled her hours when she wasn't spending time praying for others.

One day when we were talking, Mom shared with me that she was feeling so useless. She was looking for a way to feel like she still had some value to this world. We had been talking about intercessory prayer when I found myself saying, " Mom, maybe your mission in life now is to pray for the many people that you know. You have more time to spend in prayer than you have ever had." It made me feel so good when she responded positively and even excitedly about having a mission. I could picture her, sitting in her chair praying and then drifting off for a heavenly little nap.

I would think about her as I was going about my daily chores. I remembered thinking, when I still had both my parents, that I couldn't imagine being without them. Yet, how could I wish for someone I loved as much as I loved my mother, to continue to live with such terrible arthritic pain? She was never ashamed to admit that there were times when she became impatient for Heaven to become a reality. The doctors and the nurses at the "Home" had done all they could to make her as comfortable as possible. I was feeling quite helpless!

Because of a lack of education, Mom's life had been one of much hard physical work which had really taken a toll on her body. She had also been known as the "organizer" in our church community. If no one else felt that they could do the job, Mom was always counted on to get the work done. Now it was very apparent that Mom was the one who needed help. I guess in a strange way it was her turn to be on the receiving end.

Many of us considered her to be a real survivor. She had lived through the deaths of her parents, a brother, her in-laws, a grandson, a son, and then the final blow – the death of her husband. I wondered why surviving had to be so tough? Work, toil, love, give, and then end up basically helpless and in great pain during life's ebbing years. Other senior citizens traveled and fellowshiped with one another, or relaxed and enjoyed some of the good things in life. My mother couldn't even travel to my home for a visit.

As I journaled thinking about my parents, I was so thankful realizing that I wouldn't even be here if they hadn't given me life. I wouldn't have the character or be the person I am if they hadn't shaped and molded me. They were wise enough to know when to let go and let me direct my own future. The greatest gift Mom and Dad gave their children was bringing us to the Baptismal Font as infants. They kept those promises made before God, and we grew in our faith, keeping that faith as adults.

Then the day came when I got that phone call from the nursing home. We are sending your mother to St. Croix Hospital by ambulance; she is having a hard time breathing. I left as quickly as I could to be with her. When the doctor came to check on her, he also talked with me. He really didn't think there was much chance that she would make it through the night. She had congestive heart failure. Even though Mom had previously stated to her family that she wanted to be kept comfortable but she did not want any life support intervention, the doctor wanted me to double check with her. I didn't want to, but I was told that I had to so it could be noted in her chart. Several friends and relatives visited that evening.

I was told that I could stay overnight in the small family waiting room with a choice of a sofa or recliner to sleep on. Because my mom was a fighter, I stayed in that waiting room for many nights. One night when I was trying to rest, I took my pencil and paper and I wrote the following prayer.

Lord, My Lord;

You have given each one of us this marvelous machine called our body. You breathed the breath of life into it, and it gives us our being. We can abuse it, and it forgives us. We can hurt our body, and it gathers its forces to heal itself. It can endure illness and disease for an incredibly long time.

Just when we think that it can't possibly keep on sustaining life, the body puts its armies to work to keep fighting the battle. Yet, Lord, I sometimes wonder – why?

My mom has so much pain and now her lungs and heart are failing. Her body heaves with each breath. She doesn't eat. She is so sick.

If this is to be her last illness, then Lord, please take her home soon. Don't let her just linger to continue suffering.

Let her, Lord, be at peace and at rest in your bosom. She loves you. She's not afraid of passing to the next life. She says that her bags are packed and her ticket is bought. She is just waiting for her trip to begin.

So Lord, if all she has ahead of her for this life is pain, please let her start her trip so she can experience eternity with you.

Thank you for hearing me, Lord. Amen

Mom did get moved back to the nursing home and was placed in the Skilled Care Unit. I followed the ambulance as we made our way back. She seemed to rally for a while, and I made the trip up there every few days.

One Saturday when I was there, a friend, Elsie, and her mother, who we called Grams, came to visit. By then Mom had basically quit eating. I would spoon-feed her juice and other liquids. We were not sure if she knew that Elsie and Grams were there. It was good for me to see them, and they did talk to Mom. Even though she was too weak to acknowledge them, I think she knew they were there. I stayed until 9 PM that day. I just didn't want to leave. However, the head nurse, Sue, assured me that Mom could go on like this for several days. We would keep in touch, and she would call me immediately if things worsened. I was torn because I had this feeling that I really needed to get some things done at home. So, I left promising that if I didn't hear from them, I would be back on Wednesday.

The morning of Wednesday, May 25, 1988 dawned. I wondered if this would be the day that Mom would get on her bus to go "home" as she would say. Her bus was death to her earthly body, and her home was Heaven. As she stated many times, "Christ has bought my ticket and my bags are packed; I'm just waiting for my journey to begin."

I had promised I would visit her on that day so I proceeded to send my children to school and my husband to work. I needed to quickly do some business; and, then, I would be on my way. But what would I do about this terrible headache?

I decided to take some aspirin and set the alarm clock to go off in one hour. I had lain down for a while. However, I did not sleep; I just peacefully rested even though a little voice kept repeating, "Take some nice clothes along for your mother."

Many of her things had been stored at our house for several weeks. I knew there was only one reason for me to bring her clothes. My headache had disappeared so I got up, calmly chose two outfits and put them in my car. I didn't try to make sense out of why I did it; I just did it. I was now becoming somewhat anxious to be on my way even though I had not received a call from the nursing home.

I kept getting delayed, and I did not get to Mom's until 1 PM. Sue, her nurse, said, "Kay, things are not good with your Mom, but she is waiting for you." They had started to call me and assumed that since I did not answer I was on my way. She was lying on her bed very peacefully; but I was shocked to see that her hands and arms were blue; and she seemed to be starring into space. Her body was cold to the touch even though her temperature was very high. I knew immediately that this was indeed the day that Mom would get her wish and reach her heavenly home. I called the office of the contractor that Cy worked for and asked that he call me as soon as possible. My intention was for him to come up to be with me that afternoon.

Stroking her hair, I said, "I love you, Mom." I recited the 23rd Psalm for her and she blinked her eyes. My spirits rose and I said, "Mom, if you heard me say the 23rd Psalm and you know that it is me, please blink your eyes again. She blinked again. I hugged her as much as I could and held her hand knowing that she knew I was there. I will never forget that moment! God was there, too, in a very special way.

Mom's sister, Myrtle, came; and I relayed the eye blinking incident to her. She then spent a few moments with Mom. As we both stood there caressing her, she took a quick deep breath; and after a moment I asked Myrtle to find Sue. "I think that breath was her last one," I said.

She was so quiet and so peaceful. Sue confirmed that Mom no longer needed to breathe. Myrtle and I hugged knowing that she was at home at last. Her room in heaven had been prepared, and now she was occupying it. The phone rang. It was Cy; so I told him it was over and asked him to come right away. Sue allowed my aunt and me to stay with Mom for a while. When the nurses did move her, there was no pain – she was so peaceful. The moment was joyful in the midst of deep sadness.

Sometime later I delivered to the funeral home one of the outfits that I had been instructed by that "little voice" to bring with me when I left home that day.

dw

Dad(Harold) and Mom(Esther) Nelsen

Chapter Two

Health Challenges On Our Road

"The Lord is my strength and my song; he has become my salvation!" Psalms 118:14

Gwen is a rather new friend of mine. I have been blessed to become her friend and to appreciate the gifts that God has given her. One gift that is evident very quickly after meeting Gwen is that of humor. She finds something funny in the most ordinary things in life, and she has a wonderful way of laughing at herself which makes the rest of us laugh too. After spending time with Gwen, my body feels cleansed and refreshed from laughing with her.

There came a time when humor would become a lifeline for Gwen. In fact, it may have been that her very life depended on her ability to find something funny in the midst of a very serious fight for her life. This is her story as she told it to me.

"I need Gwen! Where is Gwen?"

My Detour for Cancer
Gwen's Story

I was diagnosed with rectal cancer in September 1998. I had
known that things weren't right for a couple of years. The humor in
my story starts right in the beginning. I had always been a very
modest person, and I was so afraid to go for a checkup because I
didn't want anyone to see my body. I was too modest to even see a
foot doctor. Would you believe that the cancer was the worst place
that it could possibly be? Consequently, I didn't admit it or talk about
it to anyone; but, I knew in my heart that something was very wrong.
I just kept hoping that I was mistaken.

My husband, Bill, our son, Mike, and I went on a trip in August
with California as our destination. When we got to Colorado, we hit
very heavy weather with tornadoes in the area. After the storms
passed we continued on our way. We were winding through the
mountains west of Denver when our motor home broke down. We
ended up at a campground in Glenwood Springs, CO and had a very
difficult time finding someone to make the repairs. The fuel pump in
the gas tank had broken. We couldn't go anywhere for several days
because the parts had to be brought in from Chicago. The good thing
was that our son, Mike, and I had a lot of time together while the
repairs were being made. It was like God knew that I would treasure
that special time. We spent a lot of time in the local K-Mart and went
to the movies. Meanwhile, Bill kept checking for parts and bugging
the repair garage. When the parts finally came, it was nearly quitting
time on Friday; and Bill had to convince the mechanic to make the
repairs before he left for the night to get his liquid supper at the local
pub. In addition, the next day was Saturday; and the mechanic didn't
work weekends.

After leaving Glenwood Springs we stopped at a Perkins
Restaurant in Grand Junction for supper. In the parking lot we
noticed gasoline leaking from our motor home. So we started trying
to locate a repair shop but had no success. Finally, an angel appeared
in the form of a tow truck driver who knew someone he could get to

look at our problem. That second angel found the gas line had not been properly re-attached to the gas tank. He fixed the problem and wouldn't even take any money for it. We finally arrived at our California destination, but our time for touring was severely shortened.

After returning home I had no choice but to tell Bill that I was really hurting. He told me that he could tell because I had rested a lot on the trip. He insisted that I go to the doctor immediately. I promised him that I would first-thing in September.

Even though I had been so scared for a long time, I now knew I had no choice but to have a physical. I got into see Dr. Mayer (my personal doctor) promptly, and she seemed pretty positive about the diagnosis. I don't even remember if she actually said that I had cancer. She quickly set up an appointment with a cancer specialist, Dr. Tony Hecht. He then set up many more tests. One that I needed was a colonoscopy because by now they knew there was a big problem. He had a marvelous way of making me relax; he was funny, and we could laugh together. Can you imagine laughing before a colon test?

It was at this point that many things in this whole saga started to go wrong. They put me to sleep to do the colon procedure, and then the patient scheduled before me started having heart problems. They had to deal with him and just let me wake up. Of course, they had to put me back to sleep again later to do the test.

I was told that the next procedure would be an ultrasound which was promptly scheduled. A little later I was called and told that there was a change. It was explained to me that they were booked but that there was a big medical convention taking place and this could be a part of a teaching time. Unless I did it this way, I would have to wait a couple of weeks. I couldn't wait; so I reluctantly agreed.

The doctors were in another room during the procedure watching everything on a screen. There was a woman strategically positioned in the exam room with a movie camera. Yikes! I looked at the screen, and I saw what looked like a Great White Whale; and I decided I wasn't going to watch anymore. I was thinking, "Sure, OK. I wasn't brave enough to go to one doctor and now doctors from all over the world were focusing on me. Remember how modest I am. I just had to laugh about how things were turning out."

When the procedure was done, the doctor said, "Mrs. Couch you will have to have a colostomy, and it will not be reversible." I guess that's when it really hit me; even though I had known in my heart for a long time that I had cancer. I cried, but not for long.

He continued, " Mrs. Couch, you have to have the surgery or you will die."

I said, "No, no." I wasn't disagreeing with him, it was just my way of saying no for the whole situation that I was finding myself in. I had just had my worst fears confirmed.

Within the hour I was talking to my surgeon, Dr. Buls, a quiet man from Australia. He asked me how soon I could schedule surgery. I told him that my son was being confirmed on Sunday the 20th, and I wanted to do it after that. The date was set for the 22nd. As I was leaving, I asked him, "Will I be able to dance and to go swimming afterward – after the surgery?"

Then Dr. Buls replied, "Yes, you will." Then I shocked him by replying, "Oh great, because I can't dance and I can't swim now." He was a very serious man and he looked at me sort of funny. However, humor was the only way I could handle this. I thought about all the other activities I would be able to do – maybe sing and run marathons?

I didn't want to tell my Pastor yet because I knew that when I looked in his eyes I would see his caring and compassion, and I wasn't ready for that. I also didn't want anyone in my congregation to know. I just didn't want to be the focus of attention and have people feel sorry for me on Mike's Confirmation Day. I wanted this to be Mike's special day.

Mike and his friend, Joanna, served communion on Confirmation Sunday. We noticed that Joanna was crying a little bit which brought my tears and then Bill's. No one knew the real reason. They just thought it was tears of joy because of the special day it was. I had told Bill, my mom and Dad, and my kids. What I didn't know was that Bill had also told Pastor Simpson. His family had made me feel so loved without letting on. God kept sending me angels that I wasn't even aware of. My mother graciously had the confirmation party because she knew that I wasn't feeling well and was short on energy. Besides, our septic needed to be pumped which made it a perfect excuse to have the party at her house.

From the very start of going to the doctors and specialists, things kept happening that were sometimes nothing but bizarre. When I had to drink that gallon of stuff before my colonoscopy, I went into the bathroom only to find that the electricity had gone off. When there was no electricity the plumbing didn't work right either. It was quite a joke – I had to be careful of water use and I had to sit in the bathroom with a flashlight. If it was going to happen to anyone, of course it would be me! Wouldn't you know that as soon as I was done in the bathroom, the lights came back on.

I went into the hospital on Tuesday the 22nd. Pastor Simpson called me on Monday. He asked how I was, and then he made another comment that indicated to me he knew. I was glad that he did.

I had to be at the hospital early to be measured for the stoma bag. They have specially trained nurses to do that. But I didn't know anything about it; and, of course, I had to be silly. I told her that I was afraid I wouldn't be able to see it good enough. With age and gravity the stoma had better be placed high enough for me to reach it. She was the nicest lady, and she assured me that she knew what she was doing. I then found out that Pastor Simpson had come to the hospital; so we went to the chapel to pray and to visit a while.

I was eager to have the surgery although it ended up being very extensive. Besides the colonoscopy, I also had a hysterectomy because of large fibroids and a hernia that needed to be repaired. The cancer was a stage two. I can't blame anyone but myself for it going so far. When I was waking up from the surgery, Bill was standing beside me and he said, "You had a hysterectomy." I looked at him and I thought, "Yeah right, OK." I really thought he didn't even know what he was talking about. Of course, I found out later that he was right.

I knew God was with me. I always talked to him in my mind and prayed all the time. Of course before the actual diagnosis, I had prayed, please don't let this be true. Then when it was diagnosed as cancer my prayer was simply, "Help me handle it." I wanted to see Michael grow up because he was just in 8th grade. I wanted to be around for him. The other children were grown, and I had grandchildren; but they still had their families. I didn't read my Bible just then, I mainly talked to God. After my first set of Chemotherapy treatments, I was so ill that I couldn't pray. I felt terrible about it. I would get the Bible out, but my vision was blurred. I was just too sick.

One day Lu Ramberg called me. I didn't really know her that well. I had seen her in church and talked with her a few times. However, I confided in her that I couldn't pray. She was the first person that I had told. She said that it was OK because the Holy Spirit would pray for me. She gave me a Bible verse and read it to me over the phone. It is from *Romans 8:26*, "In the same way, the Spirit helps us in our weakness. We do not know what we ought to pray for, but the Spirit himself intercedes for us with groans that words cannot express." Lu put my fear to rest.

When I got home, my mother would sit with me all day and my dad would often come too. I had to get used to wearing an appliance, and I was really weak from the surgery. However, a month after surgery Michael had been chosen to be in a special Wisconsin State Honors Choir and had to travel to Madison for a big event. We really wanted to go to hear the choir sing. So, even though it was a big undertaking, we did just that. Of course, I rested a lot in the motel room; but I did get to go to the concert. That was great! I remember how beautiful the faces shone, the music sounded and the food tasted. I don't remember being upset about the negative happenings; I was only curious as to what was going to happen next.

My therapy seemed to be so much different than everyone else's. I was always the exception. It seemed that whatever shouldn't happen did happen. I was not supposed to lose my hair from the kind of chemotherapy they gave me, but I did. My mother would try to clean up the loose hair as it fell out. One day as she vacuumed my pillow, I took the hose and vacuumed my head. She was shocked! I have told this to other cancer patients and they have laughed. In some cases they vacuumed their heads too. "I vacuumed today" has taken on a whole new meaning.

I had unexpected reactions from therapy all along. I had to see Dr. McQuire for a pre-radiation exam. The nurse gave me a gown and told me to undress and put it on. I was so nervous that day that I told the nurse I didn't want to undress. She said that she would stay and help me. In my confusion I was trying to get my clothes off and my gown on at the same moment. I was taking off my sweater with one hand and holding my gown with the other trying to keep myself covered. I forgot, of course, that I had both my glasses and my wig on. As I was trying to perform this feat, my wig and glasses both flew across the room. So, I'm standing there half-naked, blind and bald. As the nurse picked up my belongings she said to me, "Gwen, you really must think about what you are doing." When I wanted my wig back, she assured me that the doctor wouldn't care. However, I insisted that she let me keep on my heavy socks and the boots that I was wearing – a woman has to have some dignity, you know. After the exam was over I realized that when the Dr. had come, I was half-naked under the gown wearing heavy socks and boots; and, of course, I was also bald. I think I laughed all the way home.

As Christmas was nearing, Bill insisted on taking me shopping for presents one day. So, of course, I pulled on my wig and then a hat over it. I guess neither one of them fit me very well because a lady (who was an acquaintance of my husbands) asked sweetly, "Your hat is a little crooked, may I fix it?" I couldn't believe it when she turned both the hat and the wig about 180 degrees. That meant my bangs had been hanging down on my neck. We laughed and laughed all the way to the car.

The confusion from the medicine and chemo made life interesting at times. One day I tried to write Christmas Cards. It took all day to write six of them. When Bill came home, he found that five of them were to the same person. During chemo, however, my vision was blurry; and I remember writing on a piece of paper, "Help me God."

When I was getting chemotherapy shots, I would get nauseous; and then I would get another shot for that. Chemotherapy also caused little cuts in my digestive system – from my mouth all the way down to my stoma. It was so painful that I had to swallow a liquid that would deaden my mouth and throat so I could eat. It was then that I began to struggle with exhaustion. I just wanted to stay in bed. My dad would come over and encourage me and help me to walk. He would explain, "Just walk once more down the hallway – add one more trip each day." That time I was so sick, that I had gone into a state of depression.

The turning point from depression came when I had an appointment with Dr. Hecht. He made such a difference by saying to me, " Get a life, Gwen." He went on to talk to me about my life and everything that I had to live for.

"Me, have a life!" I was thinking. I really didn't expect to have a "life" again. Then I remembered how I used to tell my kids to "get over it." Soon after that, Bill came home with tickets for Las Vegas, Nevada. My parents were going down to meet my aunt and uncle in Vegas the next day. So, Bill decided we were going to go down on an earlier flight and surprise them all at the airport. They were very surprised and couldn't believe their eyes when they saw me. Yes, I had to rest often; but I was again enjoying doing things that healthy people do. I went to breakfast with them and even visited. When we got home, I started seeing a few people occasionally.

When I went to the Cancer treatment center in Maplewood for radiation treatments, everybody was so kind. The patients were very sick, some were skinny, some were in wheelchairs, some were bald, some were very old; but I never saw one person cry. It was amazing because you would think that everybody would be down. The spirit was wonderful!! God was working in so many people and the nurses were like angels. It wasn't sickening sweetness; it was like we were just regular people – we weren't treated like we were sick or different. That was kind of neat because when you are sick, you aren't like everybody else; but you want to feel normal. I had so many laughs there; we seemed to be able to joke about everything. Some patients would just be quiet and prefer not to talk. If there was anyone who did happen to be a little down, the nurse would say, "Here sit over by Gwen; she will cheer you up." I found I could even tease a little. Radiation was different because my mind was clear again. When my friend, June, said that she would drive me for one of the weeks (I went every day), it was winter and I knew she was not looking forward to it – she was apprehensive. The second day she took me, the nurse already knew her name.

During radiation I had a reaction, which was very serious, and I was hospitalized again. My immune system was so weak that I ended up with an infection as well as a twist in the intestine. When I had regained enough strength, I decided to go for a walk one day. I soon met a clown in the hallway. It was actually a woman who had been Klondike Kate for the St. Paul Winter Carnival. She was wondering where a particular room was, and I told her that I would take her there. I was really glad when my nurse saw us because, otherwise, I am sure that she would never have believed me if I had told her that I was just talking and walking with a clown. One of the nurses and I had fun joking each day. It's amazing how God had sent Rosemary to me. We could have had a vaudeville act – we just clicked!

I was in the hospital quite a few days that time. At one point when I was having a lot of pain, it was decided I should have the intestinal test where I had to drink some white, chalky stuff. They would x-ray me; I would have to drink some more; then I would repeat the whole process. They pushed me in a wheelchair down this very long cold tunnel to the x-ray room. They gave me a couple of warm sheets to wrap around myself. I put them up around my head too. They asked if I was still cold. When I told them that I was, they gave me a couple more sheets. I looked like an authentic Egyptian mummy. They must have thought that I was too weak to walk because they helped me out of the wheelchair and up on the table.

While they were moving me, I said, "If my wig falls on the floor don't kick it away – it's only my wig, not some sort of animal." After this up and down process was repeated a couple of times, I asked them if I could just push my own wheelchair. They looked at me rather shocked and surprised and said, "You mean you can walk by yourself?"

I replied, "Yes," and I left the exam room pushing my chair and carrying all my own blankets. I was the only patient who had the royal treatment. The others didn't even have a blanket.

They then gave me a rest from treatments for a while after which I was given another round of chemo along with the radiation that had to be started all over again.

You know that verse about all things working together for those who love God? Well, I believe that was happening. You see, the timing was unique because Dad was diagnosed with lung cancer six months after I was diagnosed with my cancer. His was already metastasized. It was so devastating for all of us! However, I really knew what he was going through. We could sit and talk and be with each other in a deeply spiritual way. I could relate to everything he shared with me. Our relationship became even closer and deeper, and I appreciated how he had been there for me when I was going through the worst of the surgery and the treatments. I would do my best to encourage him. The experience that we shared was worth my being so ill. I would have been more frightened for him if I wasn't going through it too. Now I was asking him if I could help him walk. My dad lost his fight in September of that year – one year after I was diagnosed.

I went to therapy class one day even though I was worried about Dad. A lady was there not because she had cancer but just because she thought that she would get it. She was depressed and crabby. The people who had had cancer weren't like that. They were a joy to be around. Another sweet lady said that she was supposed to lose her hair, but she really wanted to keep it until after a luncheon that she had to go to. So, I told her about vacuuming my head; and she laughed. The next time we met she said that she had used the vacuum that day.

I have never been angry about having cancer because I now see blessings that have happened. My cancer gave people the

THROUGH THE DEEP WOODS

opportunity to do good things, like sharing my pain and giving me joy. They ministered to me. I, in turn, was able to bring joy and laughter into the lives of other people also experiencing what I was going through.

In the family that I grew up in, we loved each other dearly; but we never really hugged much. Bill's family was the same way. I now feel closer to my family and especially to my husband, Bill. I now say good things to people, and I even hug them because I don't want to hold back. I couldn't do that before. It's also been a learning time for both my children and my grandchildren. They have learned not to be afraid. You see, I was so scared of cancer that I thought you could almost give it to someone else. It was such a frightening disease to me that I was afraid if people knew I had cancer, they wouldn't want to be around me. However, after I was diagnosed, the surgery and all the treatments just became a means to get well again.

I feel that God allows adversity and disease to teach us and help us grow. At fourteen years old Mike had to go to the drug store for me on a regular basis to get my medicines. The druggist got to know him by name. Ultimately, Mike ended up working at that drug store.

I am now well into my five-year window of being able to say that I am cured. I have gone back to my job, and I am involved in church. I also take care of my grandchildren quite often. Recently, I learned about spiritual gifts and found out that one of mine is that of mercy. I can now see how God allowed me to use that gift in my encounters with other patients during my illness. I am also grateful that I can laugh at myself. There were certainly lots of times for me to do that. We are told that laughter is healing, and a little sense of humor can go a long ways. I believe it was one thing that made this detour in my life much more bearable.

dw

Susan Erickson has been a friend of mine for many years. She is a writer, and I asked her to tell us her story. She has personally written about her special son.

Facing the Challenge
Our Special Son, Danny
by *Susan Erickson*

When I think back on my life with an autistic child, I realize that I have many stories to tell – some good – some not so good. Whether good or not, life with my son tells its own story of joy, tears, lessons learned, habits unlearned, and life relearned. I may often ramble; yet, I feel compelled to tell my stories whenever I can. I have a son who's mind is a mass of ramblings so maybe as I attempt to express the challenges we have faced, you will get a picture of the disjointedness that happens in the autistic mind – the mind of one who is continually challenged to make sense out of even the simplest aspects of the lives the rest of us make so complicated.

In the beginning we thought it would be so easy. Just lots of love, which we certainly had to give, and guidance…everything else would fall in place. We'd have a normal family – a happy well-adjusted son – and life would move on as planned. We really didn't understand what was ahead for us. In fact, we were clueless. Danny was 17 months old when he came to live with us, the son of mentally impaired parents, who themselves were unable to care for him (they had tried.) We knew there might be problems, but with help from available services, prayer, and love, Danny would grow as all normal children with natural curiosity abounding, pranks to play, love to give, and all the normal things that kids do to grow up in a world as crazy as this one can be. So we ventured out, becoming the adoptive parents of a beautiful brown-eyed toddler named Daniel Erick – or as we call him, Danny.

By the time Danny was two years old, we knew that we had met a challenge we hadn't exactly bargained for. He was an extremely fussy child, seeming to never want to leave my side. As long as I held him, he was fine. Often I would find myself tiptoeing around the house so that he wouldn't realize I was there. That way he'd possibly play by himself. Playing, to him, was stirring cotton balls with a wooden spoon in a plastic bowl or lining fuzz balls, pulled from his blanket, along the floor. This eventually evolved into hours of lining up marbles on the floor (when he was older and would no longer put them in his mouth) or unraveling his socks, usually a pair a day. Creative play, as we knew and judged it, just wasn't there for him. He didn't seem to care about the toys we gave him, and books were a nuisance in his little mind. His greatest comfort came in holding a cotton ball in his hand wherever he went. Nighttime was usually rough with lots of non-stop noise making, head banging, or curling his hair in knots on the back of his head. He would wake in the night screaming and inconsolable. Never, could we go to comfort him. Our attempts at comforting only threw him into a greater frenzy. Screaming, he would thrash around in his bed from end to end until my husband would, in a very firm voice, tell him to quiet down. Then he would suddenly stop, lay down and go back to sleep. There were the periods of time as he got older when he would leave his bed and sleep on the hard floor or in the closet, not caring to seek the comfort and warmth of his soft bed

Behavior after behavior became more unconventional and bizarre. People would tell us, "Don't worry so, he's just in his terrible two's." The terrible two's went into the terrible three's and four's and five's – never really ending. At three years old, we decided that regardless of what everyone else was saying, we would have Danny tested. These things he did were not normal, and in our hearts we knew this. We already had a six year old daughter, and nothing compared. The tests proved our fears. Danny was diagnosed with "Pervasive Developmental Disorder with Autistic Tendencies" – IQ untestable. That label eventually became straight Autism – IQ still untestable. Behavior wasn't the only aspect of this disability. Danny had cognitive/communicative problems, obsessive compulsive disorder, and possible bi-polar disorder. Language was difficult, constantly contributing to both his and our frustrations. He'd have one thing on his mind – we'd have something else on ours, and we couldn't find ways to get it across to each other. This would often result in anger, temper tantrums, or just plain tears on both our parts. And for Danny it resulted in even more bizarre behavior. We learned soon enough a fact that will always be a significant part of Danny's life. His skills for rational reasoning and good judgment are severely impaired. I'm not saying they're totally missing, but impaired enough that Danny will never be able to live safely on his own in a non-supervised environment.

But don't be fooled by Danny's actions, communication barriers, and behavior impairments. He was (still is) one very clever boy. I'd say smarter than average in learning about people…what buttons to push…what tactics to manipulate. To Danny negotiation became the name of the game. He's still the best in the business. Many who have disabled children will find themselves saying, "Don't ever underestimate the abilities of your disabled child…just when you think you're on top of what they're doing or two steps ahead of them, you realize, in actuality, that you're already two steps behind." And you don't even know how it all happened. Danny was a master at slight of hand, distracting, and confusing the victim. Yes, as a matter of survival, we had to learn how to be as clever as he, always anticipating what his next tactic would be, and failing miserably on more occasions than I'd even like to think of.

Danny is now 20 years old. He lives in a group home, and is, without a doubt, the highest functioning resident in the group home. He has worked hard in his own way to conquer his life's barriers. He realizes in a very nad've way that he is different and that he needs help to work his way through this life. He oozes with charisma; and although, his communication methods are not up to our standards, he does a beautiful job of bringing people into his life and heart. Often, I have felt that he has an insight into God and the universe that is far beyond what the cluttered mind of the normal individual can grasp. I'm proud of Danny for these skills. He has a childlike innocent faith that many of us challenge and lose when we reach our 20's. He believes in Santa Claus, the Easter Bunny, and God and refuses to let anyone tell him otherwise. In fact, annually he has his picture taken with the Easter Bunny and then proudly displays it on his dresser for that year.

Always, I prayed for Danny to be normal...to have a normal life...to be accepted. That was in the beginning. Then, I knew that wasn't going to happen. I never blamed God. I never blamed anyone really. I just began to accept that Danny was who he was and that we needed to be proud of him for whatever it was he could accomplish in life, no matter how trivial it seemed to us. I learned through the years that Danny was brought to us as a special gift – not to just my husband and me, but to all who came in contact with him. I began to see just how he so dramatically influenced the people around him with his outgoing innocent greetings. His ability to make people smile when he'd say "Hello, Happy New Year" and it was already March. I saw how he tested our patience and our abilities to learn creative approaches to behavior that was unacceptable and abnormal to us. With Danny I had to learn to look at the reasons why he was doing what he was doing and not just jump into the situation with anger and inappropriate responses. I saw for the first time in my life that if I was going to help Danny be the best he could be, I had to be the best I could be. I learned patience from Danny beyond any I ever dreamed I would be capable of. I felt good about that because I knew that was one of my major shortcomings. But best of all, I learned to see things with a sense of humor. If I couldn't laugh at the many bizarre situations we faced, I would fold up and wither away. We needed to laugh and still do.

As I look at my 20 year old son now. I don't know where he is going (do any of us know that about our 20 year old children?) But I do know where he has been and what he has already done in his short life. He has been a teacher. I believe with all my heart that is why God gave the world Danny. He has taught each person he has touched their own lessons of love, patience, tolerance, laughter, and much more. He has influenced some to make working with the disabled a career. And he has brought to those he's touched a lasting impression of the beauty found in those who are different.

It has been said that the Autistic person is one who is standing on the edge of the universe never quite daring to step inside, always observing but remaining isolated on the periphery. In a sense this is true. Try as we may, we cannot reach into Danny's very complicated mind to see how he is thinking, why he thinks that way, what his motives are, what hurts him, what doesn't hurt him, or how he perceives himself. I always got the impression that Danny thought he was alright about himself. His self-esteem was right up there, but other times I'm not so sure. Every day of my life I worry about Danny. I wonder if I have done the right things for him. I chastise myself when I show irritation toward him. I feel good when he is happy. I cry when he is out of sorts. I know we were meant to be mother and son in no uncertain terms – this was no coincidence; and I know that God is and always has been there to guide us through to make sure that the lessons are being taught and learned, one by one.

Danny will continue asking "what reason…" after every statement I make. He'll continue wanting to know how many runways are at all the airports in the world and following his question with, "what's your best guess?" He'll continue wanting to know what I want to come back as in my next life and at the same time remembering all his dead aunts and uncles and commenting on how much he misses them. He'll continue being curious about things that the rest of us would never even dream of thinking about. And we will continue being perplexed and confused by each question he asks. But, you know what, that's Danny and that won't change. And God will always be there to remind me of that and provide me with the strength to cope with whatever Danny and I need to face. The challenge is there and the challenge will be met.

dw

The New Year's Gift
Danny's Sunday

by *Susan Erickson*

December 30, just another Sunday. The two of us head for church. Danny has only one real reason for going to church and that's to "Share the Peace." It's his time to shine. When the pastor says, "Let's share the peace," Danny is up and shaking hands with as many people as five minutes can allow. Ever since our Pastor mentioned in one of his sermons that all people are 'neighbors,' Danny has been convinced that greeting everyone is a must for living right.

Our Sunday ritual continues after church with lunch at one of Danny's favorite restaurants. In his mind, we must patronize only the few restaurants he has meticulously chosen as worthy. There is little room for change. It's OK – Sunday is Danny's day. Eating, to Danny, is a serious event and not considered a leisurely activity. So when Danny is done, well, that means we're both done and ready to meet our next adventure. Again, there are only a few favored activities; and Danny presents these week in and week out as our only options. They can be changed but only through careful planning by Danny himself.

On this Sunday, the choice is to go to the airport. Danny does understand that since 9-11 we can no longer watch airplanes from the airport observation deck. He has accepted this alteration with as much calm and grace as he can possibly handle. With his creative mind actively at work, he has found a very viable alternative to the airplane watching ritual; and this one has an added perk. It's the airport observation parking lot. Not only can Danny watch airplanes, but also, he can wave to all the cars that pass, with the one and only reward being a wave returned.

The ritual in the airport parking lot goes like this. Mom (that's me) finds the parking space the furthest away from all other cars just to keep from attracting undo attention. Danny stands outside the car (regardless of the Minnesota temperature.) I prefer the warmth of the car where I can read; listen to the radio; and, yes, sleep. Danny likes this arrangement best: I'm safe in the car and less likely to interfere with his activities. There we are: Danny in the freezing cold watching planes and waving to every passing car and me, warm and comfortable inside. He's in his element – his place of serenity and joy. Danny is happy!

This particular Sunday, it's very cold. Having parked in the usual non-conspicuous spot, I begin centering my world on the fascinating book I'm reading. I know Danny's safe. He's right in front of the car where I can see him all the time. After 45 minutes of blissful reading, I happen to look up. To my surprise and irritation there is a car parked on either side of me. I think to myself, "Why do you people have to park so close when you have the whole lot to choose from?" Then I get nervous thinking that maybe we're being watched by airport security or FBI, "What have we done this time?" As these thoughts roll through my mind, the woman in the black town-car on my right approaches my car. Without warning, she opens my car door on the passenger side and hands me a folded sheet of notebook paper. I'm stunned and apprehensive. She asks me to take it. I hesitatingly decline, thinking that it's a complaint about Danny that I won't want to read. But then she says it again, "It's OK, please take it." She seems sincere enough so I take it, open it, and begin reading:

I learned a good lesson today after watching a young man with what I would say mental challenges – That is until I watched him. You see he was standing out in 16° degree weather waving at every car that passed by. As he waved he smiled and was extremely happy if someone waved back. How simple…His human contact of just a wave in return was all he needed to be happy. Such a simple act, brought such joy. When was the last time I waved at someone? (other than him) When was the last time I simply greeted a stranger? I was sad today about a lot of things in my life – But for 10 brief minutes I was happy – every time someone waved back at this young man.

Thank You!
Jinna

Feeling ashamed of my resistance to this woman, I look up as she's pulling away in her car. I wave and smile with grateful appreciation, realizing that this woman has given me the best New Years gift ever. She has taken the time to notice the beauty and simplicity in the actions of my autistic son. She has appreciated the small gifts he so innocently brings to the people he encounters every day of his life. She has seen the teacher in him, and she has observed his human worth. I know I will probably never see this woman again. (I'd like to thank her.) Yet, she has brought into focus a life's lesson to be shared with all. She has reminded me of the invaluable worth that comes in the simple act of smiling at and greeting someone, whether friend, acquaintance, neighbor, or stranger. As Danny so wisely reminds me..."Everybody's a neighbor, mom, all over the world!"

dw

Danny at the Airport

Kimberly's Courage

I would like to introduce Kimberly to you. She is now a woman in her thirties. She has chosen a career as a legal secretary and is a single lady. The timing of her coming into our life was a real miracle.

Kimberly was born in Korea. She was placed in my arms at the airport just nine months after our eighteen-month-old son, Kyle, was taken to Heaven. Nine months is the same length of a pregnancy. By God's wonderful grace our arms were no longer empty.

Kimberly did not by any means replace Kyle, no child could. But it was wonderful to have a small child, just 16 months old in our home and in our family, to love. We had started her adoption process before Kyle's unexpected death. It took great love for her family to give up their precious Choon Mi Kim so that she could have a better life. We were the blessed parents who adopted her.

Shortly after her arrival it quickly became apparent that Kimberly's birth mother had been very malnourished; and Kimberly had also been suffering from a lack of good nutrition since her birth. She weighed just 14 lbs when she arrived in America to join our family. She felt like a feather when we held her, and it took several months to get her adjusted to good food and on her road to good health.

The results of malnutrition have been with Kimberly and will be with her for the rest of her life. Her baby teeth needed to be filled and many of them had to be capped so she could keep them long enough for her permanent teeth to come in properly. When she became a teenager she began struggling with some flexibility problems. We eventually learned that her right hip socket had never fully developed, and the joint was beginning to freeze giving her a lot of leg and knee pain. She would have to undergo a total hip replacement at the young age of 21 in order to move freely without pain. There is every reason to believe that this birth defect was due to her birth mother's malnutrition before Kimberly's birth.

Following is a prayer that I wrote and prayed on June 18, 1993 just a couple of days before her surgery.

Dear God our Creator: You created each and every one of us. You loved us so much that you even gave your only Son, Jesus, to redeem us when we were not worthy. I praise and I thank you for that.

This morning my throat is tight, my body is tense and I'm wishing that the next few days were already over. I am wanting to shield Kimberly from the ordeal that she has ahead of her. On Monday she's scheduled for a total hip replacement. It'll be at 10:30 A.M. She is being so brave – I am a real coward. I love her so much, dear God! What a gift she has been to us! I'm anxious for her to be rid of her bad limp, pain etc. I just wish that there was an easier way of doing it.

Oh, God, I know you didn't promise life would be easy – just that you would never leave us. In John 11:4 you also told Martha and Mary that Lazaras' illness was for the glory of God. May I ask, Lord, that our whole family will become closer – that your glory will be evident – that Brian, Kevin and Brenda will be touched by your hand. That they will go to you in prayer.

Continue to give Kimberly a courageous spirit. May she be sure of her salvation and of your presence with her.

Now, Lord, there's me – the uptight, nervous Mom. Be with me – relax me – assure me – touch me – and give me lots of strength! Keep Cy calm and confident and grant us, God, the ability to unite forces and to pull together for the sole purpose of Kimberly's healing.

I love you dear God, and I ask your forgiveness. Give me wisdom for decisions that lie ahead. Thank you for your promise to be with us, and may we never forget it.

In your Son's name, Jesus Christ our Savior. Amen.

Kimberly's surgery went very well. Now she can do most things that the rest of us take for granted. She is a rather private person and doesn't want her Mom writing much about her. However, Kimberly's physical challenges, which happened because of something she had no control over, remind me to be thankful every day for the gift of health.

dw

And She Danced!

Holiday TV programming seemed to bring ice-skating shows galore. Professionals were gliding around the ice interpreting the melodic strains of familiar Christmas tunes. Skaters leapt high above the ice twisting and flying through the air then gracefully landing with beauty and ease. We sat transfixed on their skill as the spirit of the Holidays filled our souls.

The music changed and the familiar strains of "Beauty and the Beast" brought a female skater to the ice twirling and dancing around and around. Then out of the corner of my eye, the dancer I saw was right in the room – I could touch her. She twirled and hopped and danced like the skater. She laughed, and we both laughed. The dancer was my daughter, Kimberly, caught up in the beauty of the moment. Now, she was experiencing freedom – freedom of movement and freedom that dance gives a person. Her imperfect hip was a beast turned beautiful by medical technology. My heart filled with music, and everything was good for a Christmas moment.

dw

Life Changing Injury

"And we know that in all things God works for the good of those who love him, who have been called according to His purpose," *Romans 8:28*. These words the Apostle Paul wrote to the Romans can be of great comfort in a time of need. When something bad happens that interrupts our life in an unexpected way, these words can certainly bring hope. In 1986 I found myself wondering what good could possibly come from a fall that would lay me up for the better part of a year?

It was early March and the snow had started to melt leaving little puddles and wet sidewalks and steps. When the night came, it would freeze leaving a virtually invisible glaze of slick ice (commonly known as black ice) over everything. One morning we were informed that it was very icy outside so I warned my children and even a neighbor to be extremely careful when they left the house.

The time came for me to gather several items that I needed to deliver. I had been careful and had put on my boots with the best soles for winter walking. I locked the house and went around the back patio breaking through some thin ice over puddles on the way. It was icy – there was no doubt about it; but I had walked and driven in these conditions many times having lived in Wisconsin and Minnesota all my life. I came to the two steps leading to the door at the back of the garage, and I stood there a moment now realizing how treacherous the ice was on those steps. I decided to move at a little angle so my whole foot would fit on the step – right foot first. In an instant I was down on the cold cement doing a split with a searing pain ripping through my right leg and knee! I changed my position and rested there a while trying to get my bearings again. I knew I had injured my knee to some extent, but it never entered my mind that I had taken the last step I would take in months. I decided that if I could get up and to the car, I would just do a couple of the important errands and then come back home and ice my leg and rest a while. Cautiously, I raised myself putting most of my weight on my left leg and then gradually some on the right leg. I was down again immediately! This time the pain was much worse than with the first fall. As a result, I felt a little light-headed and sick to my stomach. I knew, without a doubt, that my right leg was actually useless. I forced myself to concentrate on how to get help. No one could see me, and there wasn't much chance of being heard because of the block fence and yard that separated me from the street.

I had a real dilemma. Crawling was out of the question, and I found it impossible to move without the feeling that my knee was pulling apart. I was thinking clearly enough to check my pockets for my house keys and to put my gloves on. Everything else remained where it had landed. I decided to sit with my legs straight out in front of me, slide my upper body over a few inches by pushing with my hands and left leg, then reach down and bring my right leg in line with my body. Very slowly, I repeated this process over and over painfully making my way through puddles and ice water, frigid sidewalks and sharp broken ice. Even with my gloves on I managed to get some little cuts on my wrists. Finally, I reached the steps that would bring me to the kitchen where the phone was.

I honestly do not remember how I got up those outside steps and reached the lock on the door. I must have just repeated the process. I never have figured out how I unlocked the door because the handle was out of reach for me. Only God knows.

Once inside and sitting on the kitchen floor, another challenge presented itself when I looked at the telephone high on the wall. After searching around from my position on the floor, I saw a ruler that I could reach. I wound it around the phone cord and twisted it until the receiver came flying down to the floor.

Cy worked as an ironworker so I needed to call the contractors office; thankfully, I had that number memorized. I told Brenda, the receptionist, that I needed to talk to him as soon as possible because I had been injured. She, in turn, had to call the job site; and they had to find him on the tenth floor of the hotel he was constructing in downtown Minneapolis. When he called me, we decided to contact our friend who is an orthopedic surgeon instead of going to the emergency room. Cy said that he would start home immediately. When I called the Doctor's office, they told me to come in as soon as possible – the doctor we wanted to see would be leaving at noon.

The waiting for Cy to get home began. Since he was working downtown and riding the bus, I knew it could take a while for him to get home. The initial numbness lessened and the pain increased. I shivered from shock and from my cold, wet slacks; but I couldn't get off the floor. Suddenly, I became acutely aware that I needed help desperately! In one split second a freaky fall changed my life!

Over an hour after our phone conversation, Cy came through the kitchen door. In his haste he had taken the wrong bus and had walked a long ways instead of waiting for another bus. I was nervous because noon was approaching fast, and I didn't want to miss seeing this particular doctor. Cy ran to the basement to find some crutches that we had, rummaged through my clothes for dry pull on slacks, and helped me to the car. As soon as we got to the medical building, we found a wheelchair and arrived at the office just before noon.

The x-rays assured us there were no broken bones, but the examination confirmed the need for surgery. It was termed exploratory surgery because only after seeing inside would the surgeon be able to determine the extent of the injury. This was Monday and surgery was scheduled for Wednesday. My leg was wrapped and a brace put on. I was sent home to ice as much as possible and take anti-inflammatory drugs to prepare the leg for surgery. I was seated back in the wheelchair, and again helped into the car. Painkillers were prescribed and crutches became a part of my life for many months.

The day of surgery arrived with a sense of relief. I had no idea how extensive the injury was or how long the surgery would take, although I am sure my surgeon must have had some idea. It was long before MRI or other such diagnostic tools were available. Major ligament and joint repair was found to be necessary; and when I awoke my whole leg was heavily bandaged. A heavy-duty brace covered everything, and my leg was elevated. My hospital stay was five days. Before being released I had to learn how to get around on crutches, walk stairs and get in and out of vehicles. It was evident by then that healing would be a long process and require a lot of hard work and patience on my part and the part of my family.

My focus needed to change from trying to be a super mom, church volunteer, ever present parent at school activities, business woman, homemaker and wife to just learning to walk again. I basically had to switch my focus to myself, which was something that was quite unfamiliar to me at that particular time in my life. Not only did I have to change my focus, but my family was also thrust into being my caretakers. For the first couple of weeks I needed help to get out of bed and to move from one room to the other. I was only left alone for a few hours at a time. My oldest son would leave school to check on me, or a friend would come over to see if I needed help. I went from being independent to extremely dependent because of one wrong step.

I was remembered with cards, flowers, and phone calls; and several people brought over meals. Partners in my business came to help me get out orders and move some of the most important paper work from my basement office to the den of our home. I soon started physical therapy and had to depend on others for my rides until I could handle my crutches proficiently and learn how to drive using my left foot on the brake. I would place my right leg so my foot would be in position to use the accelerator, and off I would go. A stimulator was sent home with me to connect to my leg to get the atrophied muscles to respond again. The first time that I was able to lift my leg about one inch off the sofa was a joyous day. I was no longer paralyzed!

It was August before I would take my first step again. That was a victory and the beginning of getting back to a more normal life for both my family and myself. I have, in some respects, slowed down for the rest of my life because I can no longer ski or run or jump or even walk really fast; but I can walk, and for that I am grateful! As I stated at the beginning of this story, "We know that in all things God works for the good of those who love him, who have been called according to His purpose." God worked with me by teaching me some important lessons along my way to recovery.

I certainly gained a much greater sensitivity for the handicapped person – particularly my mother who at the time of my accident was crippled with arthritis. I learned how to graciously receive the wonderful gifts of help and care that many people gave me during this time. I had been taught as a child that as *Acts 20:35* says, "… It is more blessed to give than to receive." However, I also learned that there are times in our lives when we are called upon to be very gracious receivers. I was put in a situation where I needed assistance taking care of myself for several months, and it didn't matter how independent I had been before. God sent me "ministering angels" in my friends and my family to be there for me.

The physical challenges of injury or disease can set us back for quite some time, and we will find out that the world goes on without our help. That doesn't mean that what we do is worth nothing. What it does mean is that sometimes it may be wise to take stock of all the things in our lives that we think we must do. Are we enjoying each day we live and truly doing what we want to do or, are we doing what we think that everyone else expects us to do? Are we seeking God's will for our lives and asking Him to guide us in the way in which He would like us to go? Sometimes we need to be laid low for awhile so we can take the time for evaluation of our life. I may have been at that point in my life. When I think about it, I was always running.

I was slowed down, my exhausted body had lots of time to rest; and there were blessings that unfolded as my healing progressed. My "super mom" days were, thankfully, over. I was reminded once again that we could get through anything by concentrating on holding our Father's hand day-by-day.

dw

This is the story of a man who has struggled not only with the disease of Mental Illness but also with society's perception of the people who daily live with it. John has shared his journey with us through the years, and we have witnessed his struggles. He was willing to sit with me and share his story with the hope that those who read it can identify and find some encouragement. And maybe the rest of us will be less judgmental and more understanding when we come in contact with people who have this particular challenge in their life.

The Valley of Clinical Depression

In high school John was a star basketball player. He is a tall man, which was an advantage for him. Even though he loved the sport, he experienced considerable pressure because people expected him to be a high scorer at every game. In his senior year of high school, he would often wake up with his nerves on edge. Soon the doctor would be called, and John would be given a shot to calm him down. Eventually, he ended up spending a week in the hospital and was then diagnosed with Acute Anxiety Attack.

As a result of trying to lessen the stress, John chose to take a lighter load of high school class work. He continued to play basketball but was no longer a starting player. When it was tournament time, he was very happy to be in the starting lineup. John really enjoyed playing in the tournaments. He was not on medication at that time, but he was learning to deal with the stress that he would experience.

When John was in high school he thought that he was quite religious. He went to all the Lenten Services and enjoyed the sermons. In fact he even thought about becoming a pastor.

He earned a scholarship to a Lutheran College in his hometown. Once there, however, the stress increased; and he began to worry a lot about how he could manage both basketball and his studies. In spite of the worry, he stayed well and had a good freshman season averaging about 15 points at each game. In his sophomore year he played varsity and averaged about 14 points per game. As time passed, however, he found that when he was off the court, he would worry about the basketball games and would become very anxious about how he would play. In John's Junior year at college, he began to go to counseling sessions; but in spite of that help, his average dropped to 10 or 11 points a game. He even missed playing some games.

John's anxiety increased to the point that by the spring of his junior year he was admitted to the hospital for shock treatments. Those treatments took away his memory, so he has no recollection of what events actually led to his being admitted for such a drastic treatment. At that time John was diagnosed as psychotic and was often confused about who he was. He remembers thinking that he was a Native American and that he saw his grandfather. He can only remember bits and pieces and can't put them together to make any sense.

When John returned to college, he noticed that some students he had known and had considered friends would keep their distance because of the stigma that comes with having any kind of mental or emotional problems. People would ordinarily greet him, but they were awkward talking to him. John's level of anxiety made it impossible for him to complete his college courses. When he tried working, he experienced such anxiety that he needed to stop that too. In September his counselor advised him to admit himself in the state hospital as a voluntary patient. He agreed to be admitted. Though he was sane at the time, he was hoping that they could cure him of his anxiety. He absolutely did not want more shock treatments, and they assured him that their program was mostly medication and job responsibility. John worked as a dishwasher at the cafeteria. It was assumed that by giving him medication he would conquer his anxiety; however, in the next five years he was admitted three or four times and stayed three to six months each time. He did earn his college degree in 1969 by chipping away at the requirements even when anxiety made it difficult.

John was counseling with a man from Lutheran Social Services in his hometown. His Counselor had a friend who was a pastor at church in a large city whom he thought could help John. John's Dad also became instrumental in finding a vocational rehabilitation program near the church. So John moved to the city and started working part time. Eventually, he obtained a job working as a Janitor at the church. It was at that time we began our friendship with him. He continued to work part-time at the church for several years.

John struggled with low self-esteem, technically called "anxious depression." Through the years he attended church regularly, but he says that he didn't really internalize God's love. During the last five years, he says that he has grabbed hold of God's love and knows that his prayer life has become much richer and more meaningful resulting in a terrific strengthening of his faith. When he gets anxious now, he doesn't always need a counselor or a pastor; but through prayer he feels a real connection with God. There are often new challenges for him. Currently, he can't understand why he has been having some panic attacks while driving the car. Of course, he always wonders if the schizophrenia is surfacing again. This particular fear is new for him; so he just tries to relax and think about other things, which takes a lot of discipline.

John can definitely see where God had been working in his life through the years especially through support from his family, which is contrary to what was thought at one time (i.e; that the family was the cause of mental illness.) When he grew up he had a stable family who always attended church. He knows that foundation carried him through even when he didn't always realize it. Now he is blessed with a wife and two sons who love him and are there to support him.

He certainly hasn't won the battle, but the difference is that now he claims God's love; and he knows that he is not in this alone. It is interesting because recently John prayed for God to show him in a special way that He was working in his life. Soon he noticed that when he was driving and would come to a clover leaf where he needed to merge with the traffic, he would say a little prayer, "Lord, I don't know what to do, but I pray that you are with me." He would often, at that moment, see a big opening in the traffic just perfect for him to merge. It happened several times and seemed like God was giving him the assurance that he needed. These days he feels God's presence with him more than he ever has.

I remember that in 1982 John was hospitalized for three months. He told me that he was actually considered "insane." He had been married for five years by then, and they had a small child. The time in the hospital was to find a medication (it took a lot of experimentation) that would help him. In 1965 he started needing medication every day. In 1983 his Doctor was afraid that John had developed agoraphobia which means having a fear of crowds; but he knew that if John kept taking Stelazine, he could develop tardivedysknezia which is basically facial ticks. So he thought he was doing John a favor by taking him off that medication. The result was that he once again became "insane."

During his hospitalization, John remembers seeing some other friends and us when we came to visit. He also remembers some crazy things such as looking at the clothes in his closet and seeing a particular shirt that made him believe the people in the waiting area were there for his Barmitzvah. "I better get ready," he remembers thinking and then went out to the waiting area. Another time when he was watching TV and the actor started using a machine gun, he actually felt the bullets and fell to the floor. It was all so real to him. He had orange and brown clothes in his closet that actually made him think he was Hispanic.

Since then, he has had a few episodes but nothing serious. He was on Stelazine for several years, and then he was changed to Zyprexa, which is for Bipolar Depression. His diagnosis in 1983 was actually Schizophrenia combined with Bipolar Depression (experiencing high highs and low lows). The medical term is Schizo-affective-disorder. The symptoms can vary from time to time.

John now has to deal with the side effects of his medication. His continuing health problems include heart arrhythmia, rheumatoid arthritis, balance problems and the formation of blood clots. Occasional hospitalizations have been necessary to deal with these side effects.

John expressed that some of the feelings he deals with are those that other diseases can also bring such as loneliness, frustration and sadness. Trying to be of service to others is very helpful for him, but it is better if he doesn't get involved with others who suffer from similar problems. He would rather reach out to people in other situations. "Time heals" – "let go and let God." Living "one day at a time" and even one moment at a time makes things easier. He is also aware that at times the drugs affect his memory and his intellect, and sometimes he has to make allowances for that.

Often on the day of a social event, John may become very anxious even if all attending are his friends. He talks very little even at our home when others are present. He finds that it's just easier to let other people do the talking while he listens. The feelings of panic can sometimes almost paralyze him.

John has told me that he knows he is very blessed to have been married for over 25 years and to have a family. He is so appreciative of how his wife has loved him and stuck with him through the years. He says that he could well have ended up institutionalized. Nevertheless, with the help of his medications, he is able to go to church, do work around his home, visit with people, and live a fairly normal life. He lives moment-by-moment through God's grace.

He remembers how his mother embroidered the Serenity Prayer and framed it for him.

"God grant me the *serenity* to accept the things I cannot change,
The *courage* to change the things that I can change,
and the *wisdom* to know the difference."
Reinhold Niebhor

It is a prayer that has helped him travel through the valley known as mental illness.

dw

Chapter Three

Changes
In Our Path

Though our path may take an unexpected
turn, and we suddenly feel lost, God knows
where we are.

Only Glowing Embers

In the middle of a bitterly cold January night the ringing telephone jolted us from our slumber. Nervously, I answered. My cousin from Luck, Wisconsin was on the line.

Struggling for words, he simply said, "Kay, your parent's farmhouse is burning. There are fire engines there, but it looks like a total loss."

I tried to comprehend what he was saying as he assured me that my parents were safe. I quickly replied, "We'll be up there as soon as possible."

After telling Cy, we got ourselves ready and then went upstairs to our children's rooms. They were cozy and peaceful in their warm beds; but we helped them dress, and tucked them into the warming car. We had a trip of a little less than two hours ahead of us, and my need to be with my parents was growing by the minute.

The hum of the motor was hypnotizing. We were strangely silent as numbness overcame me. "The house is burning," echoed in my head.

"Please God," I pray, "Just let me wake up and find that this is only a nightmare. I just don't have the strength to go through another crisis!" Other trips because of tragedy were still too fresh in my mind.

This house that was burning was not just a house, it was the home that I grew up in. My roots were there on that farm. The sound of the spinning car wheels put me in a daze, and my consciousness filled with countless memories of a hardworking farm family that often struggled to make a living. The house was a two-story white farmhouse. A big gray wood burning furnace kept us warm when the cold winds howled through the trees on the hill where the farm buildings were clustered together. For years we had a large heat register on the living room floor, where we would huddle – each of us getting our share of the coveted warm air. Waking up on winter mornings in my upstairs bedroom, I would often be able to see my breath. I would quickly dress under the quilts so that I wouldn't freeze; and then I would dash downstairs to share, or fight for heat from the kitchen stove. I loved my big bedroom with tree branches touching a window, which revealed a broad view of the countryside. It was my own special place.

The trip seemed so long to me now. The children were peacefully sleeping and my husband was intent on his driving. My mind drifted again with thoughts of the large country kitchen. We cooked, ate, visited, did homework, had family devotions, cried and even argued there. At times that kitchen housed sick piglets and chicks as they were nursed back to health. Freshly canned fruit lined the kitchen counters in the summer. When the men came in for meals, a strange combination of odors from the barn would mix with wonderful aromas of the food my mother was serving.

I remember how Daddy would sit at that table with a dish of Cornflakes before he went to bed at night. Sometimes he was so deep in thought that he would slightly nod his head and even murmur to himself. He was probably thinking about the cow that was about to have her calf or the hay that needed to dry more before it could be put into the haymow.

I smiled as I remembered how Mom would watch for the lights to be turned off in the barn and would quickly hide behind the kitchen door. When Dad opened the door, she would sneak around it and give him a big hug. Even though there were a lot of tough times, maybe those special acts of love were part of the reason that they were married more than 40 years before Daddy died.

Somehow the two hours of travel finally passed, and we turned off the highway for the last mile on a dirt road. My stomach felt sick as we entered the driveway that went up a hill to the yard. Everyone had left including the firemen. We got out of the car and stared in breathless disbelief at what was before our eyes. All we saw was a big pile of brightly glowing embers and dirty, dirty ashes! We couldn't see much else because daylight had not yet dawned.

Our stay was short because it was important for us to go to my aunt's home where we knew that Mom and Dad would be. Her home also had a big farm kitchen, and we found some cousins had gathered there to warm up on coffee and snacks. We were greatly relieved to see that my parents were unharmed.

"We had just watched some of Johnny Carson and then gone to bed," my dad explained to us, "when your Mom heard noises in your room, Kay." He continued, "After a couple of minutes, I sat up in bed and looked out the window. The snow was bright orange, and I knew immediately that our house was on fire! I told your Mom to take her walker and start out while I called the fire department. It wasn't long before help came, including Jimmy."

My cousin, Jimmy, was a volunteer firefighter in a neighboring town. He had heard the fire call on his two-way radio. Jimmy called his brother and that's how the word spread.

We listened, asked questions, cried and hugged. Then after calling my younger brother who lived in Eastern Wisconsin, we tried to settle down for a couple of hours of very restless sleep.

Soon, much too soon, it was mid-morning; and I felt like I was in a fog. Whenever I looked at Mom and Dad, I became overwhelmed with thanks that they were survivors once again. Physically, there were few ill effects; although, their emotions were frazzled.

"Yes," I assured myself, "material things are temporary. Our lives will go on without those wonderful heirlooms from Denmark or without those pictures that we brought out and looked at occasionally. We will even survive without a beautiful memorial collage of pictures of Mark. They had been shellacked onto a large piece of wood, which was sawed off the top of a tree stump located on his land. Things can burn; but no one – absolutely no one – can take away the memories tucked carefully in our hearts."

The first order of the morning was to obtain some necessities. A trip to a clothing store was the place to begin. It wasn't long, however, before friends were bringing over things they could get along without but Mom and Dad could use. God once again sent many wonderful people to aid my parents. They stayed at my aunt and uncle's for a month and then were able to rent a house in town.

When we got back to our home in the city, I found it difficult to deal with this last blow. Maybe there had just been so many losses in the first few years of our marriage, and I was emotionally tired. Whatever the reason, I found myself angry this time. I felt I had been robbed again. The fire had stolen a part of my life.

I recalled how I used to love fires. I enjoyed the cozy feeling that a campfire gave me with the warm sweet smell of burning wood while sitting and watching the embers burn out and the light disappear. There is nothing like the taste of juicy, roasted corn and gooey toasted marshmallows. Then suddenly one January night, fire became my enemy! The coals we saw weren't welcome! The tiny flames didn't dance beautifully, and the black ashes were dirty and ugly! Fire became an awful force that couldn't be stopped until it had completely consumed its victim!

By summer the farm had been sold. It seemed as if everything from my childhood was taken from me. The memories that were so vivid to me a few months earlier seemed blurred and distant. I knew I needed to do something so I could deal with this tragedy too. I had been fighting the inevitable, but I knew that I must go back to the farm one more time.

The day for the trip had come; and in my mind's eye I pictured the house as I knew it, surrounded by big beautiful trees. I wanted to believe that the past few months were just another bad dream. Cy turned the car up the driveway; and as I looked up the hill, I wanted to cry out, "This isn't the right place! There is a new home being built here."

Wait! I do see an old friend.

It wasn't a person. It was Alis. Alis, was a very old Alis Chalmers tractor. I had learned to drive that big hunk of machinery as soon as

I could reach the clutch and the steering wheel at the same time. There it stood in tall grass with a blown out tire and rust covering the body of this old friend of mine. We had been to many fields in the area as part of threshing teams. We had cultivated fields together and had learned to bail hay with one of the first New Holland Bailers in the community. We had worked together for several years, and I was comfortable with Alis. I gave her a pat on her fender, and I bid her farewell.

My eyes went from Alis to the very faded red barn. It wasn't used anymore. How weak and lonely it looked. Once it was filled with animals and all the activity that went with them. There was that favorite cow of mine that I had named Betsy. We were buddies. One day when I was feeding her, my hayfork nicked her nose causing it to bleed. I truly think that it had hurt me more than it hurt her. The barn was always filled with cows, calves, young stock, cats and our farm dog. This barn hadn't been destroyed by fire, but it had become about as desolate as if it had.

I walked around the yard reminiscing with my family, and before long I felt the need to be alone. I wandered to the front yard that gently sloped toward the road, and I sat down on the edge of the lawn. The air seemed to fill my senses with the fragrances of the Peony and Rose bushes that once bloomed there. I began to cry so hard that my whole body shook. I turned expecting to see the tall red brick chimney that decorated this side of our house. Incredibly it was sparks from that chimney that buried themselves under wood shingles and caused the fire.

I turned back again and saw the clump of trees where my brother, Mark, and I had built a two-story treehouse one summer. Then I noticed the low spot was still there – it would fill with water in the spring and then freeze over again if we got another cold spell. Mark had driven our tractor out on that pond thinking that it was frozen solid, but both he and the tractor broke through the ice. I had raced to the house and gotten Mom who had to pull him out of that semi-frozen pond. Mark survived fine, but mom caught pneumonia and was sick for weeks. As I sat there, I was overwhelmed by the reality that I must give up my hold on this farm.

As I sat quietly, my mind seemed to relax; and I clearly heard the birds sing. The intense sadness had eased and a sense of calm slowly filled my being. My memories will always be with me even though the place where they happened had been taken away. Another family would now have the opportunity to create their own memories right here in this place.

I felt exhausted. My patient husband and children were waiting in the car. As I walked toward them, I resolved that my children would have happy memories of their childhood to tuck away and bring out when they wished. I prayed that they would have the faith to help them through the losses that they would experience in their lifetimes. As the car started down the road, the sun was shining through the windows and reminded me that, "the sun will shine again."

dw

*"Do not look forward to what may happen tomorrow;
the same everlasting Father who cares for you today
will take care of you tomorrow and every day.
Either He will shield you from suffering,
or He will give you unfailing strength to bear it."*

— *Saint Francis deSales*

Our Son Goes to War

It was his senior year of high school. Like most other classmates he was thinking about what to do after graduation. Four years of college didn't interest Kevin just then. Working? Trade school? The military? O God, please not the military.

I had always said that I never, ever wanted a child of mine to go into the military. I couldn't imagine what kind of worry that must give parents. But here we were, talking about going into military service. Kevin had already talked with recruiters who came to his school. He was deliberating between two of the Services. This was sounding a little too serious for me. I was hoping that talking with the recruiter was just a part of his decision making process, and we would really end up sending him off to college. After all, he had a steady girl friend and being gone for long periods of time wouldn't look all that attractive to him, would it?

Now this was getting scary! The Marine recruiter was sitting with Kevin at our dining room table. Then they asked me to come and join them. They wanted me to fully understand the decision Kevin had made. That's right, that's what I heard – the decision Kevin had made. "Come on now," my heart was screaming, "I was never going to have a son or daughter in the military, remember?"

They wanted me to understand Kevin's decision. That was the key – it was really Kevin's decision. It wasn't mine. We had brought our children up to be independent and that was what he was doing. He was making the choice to serve his country. Well, at least, serving his country sounded a little better. I learned that he would be doing some things with the recruiter during the summer and then would be off to basic training in California. The decision had been made; he signed the papers; he would be a Marine.

The summer passed and it was time. His Dad said good-bye to Kevin before he went to work in the morning. I took him to the airport and sat with him until it was time to board. I held him close and promised him again that we would come to his graduation from basic training in December. He walked down the jetway to the plane.

As I stood there waiting for the plane to take off, I thought back to the November 13 years earlier when we stood in this same airport waiting for a plane to arrive with our new son. He was coming from Korea. He was five years old, and he was going to be in our family. He had been sleeping so he was rubbing his eyes when we first saw him. I had thought that he was crying. My mother and father and my Aunt Myrtle were there as well as Kevin's new older brother, Brian, and younger sister, Kimberly, whom we had also welcomed into our family from Korea. In the following years Kevin became a total part of our family and as dear to us as any son could be. Here I was waving good-bye to him and thanking God that at least there was no significant war at the present time.

Kevin did not choose a particular specialty when he enlisted which meant that he would be classified in the Infantry. However, after spending several weeks in Basic Training, he called us. "Mom" he said, "they need to find someone to be a Cryptologist as well as a language interpreter. They tested 400 of us in the beginning and now there are fifty – and I'm one of the fifty." Since he wouldn't qualify as an interpreter, if he tested the highest, Cryptology would be his specialty. That would mean that he would have to pass all security clearances. Because he was adopted, he wanted me to gather all the papers including his immigration certificate and send them to him. Well, not long after that telephone call, we heard that Kevin indeed did test the highest and if he passed the security clearance, he would be serving in Intelligence as a Cryptologist. "By the way," he said, "someone from the Department of Defense will be coming to visit you." And that is just what happened late one afternoon. We had no idea when he would be coming – just that he was coming; he would also be talking to other people who knew Kevin.

Needless to say, we were quite proud of our Marine Son. We went to California for the graduation ceremonies, and it was an exhilarating experience to stand there as the National Anthem and the Marine Hymn filled the air. These graduates were now prepared to serve their country. Kevin, however, still had a year of intensive training ahead of him to qualify in Cryptology.

His girlfriend, Brenda, was now a senior in High School, and they became engaged. The following October was when the wedding was to be. We all got into the excitement of planning and preparations. Kevin would be wearing his Blues. What is it about a man in uniform, anyway? Even a mother can swoon as she looks at her son ready to march down the aisle to meet his beautiful bride. It was a beautiful wedding at Brenda's church just a few blocks from our home.

Remember that prayer of thanks I had whispered in the airport? "Thank you God that there is not a war taking place at the present time." But now a year later things were beginning to heat up in the Gulf. Kevin was finishing his intelligence training in Pensacola, FL; and that's where Brenda moved to be with him. However, it wasn't long and they where transferred to Camp LeJuene, North Carolina. It was looking like Desert Shield could turn into Desert Storm.

The tension was increasing throughout the country. The reports were not encouraging. Troops were on high alert and some were sent over in a state of readiness if needed. The New Year came, and Kevin was now a Lance Corporal. He was ready to go. "Mom," he said, "it's as if I've gone to college. I have worked very hard for my career; and I want to put those skills to use."

We had planned a couple of week's vacation in Florida and proceeded with those plans while keeping in touch with Kevin as much as possible. I can remember it as if it was yesterday. The President proclaimed that Desert Shield would now become Desert Storm. We stared at the television with our stomachs in knots knowing it was just a matter of time before Kevin would also be making that trip overseas. He would be going to that desert to serve his country. We knew there were thousands of parents feeling just as we did that unforgettable day when once again the United States was at war.

The call came soon after we arrived home. Kevin would be going into intensive Desert Storm training. He called again to say good-bye because they would not be allowed phone calls the last couple days before leaving. He would begin in infantry; and as soon as his security clearance arrived, he would be working in his specialty,

Cryptology. He promised to call us as soon as he could. I did not want that call to end. When it did, our experience of waiting and watching and praying along with countless other families began.

We joined a support group, at our church, of people who had family members serving in Desert Storm. We prayed together, and we talked about war. There were so many different and confusing opinions. I hated war. I knew that there were already so many grieving families and that grieving was not limited to just our country; the mothers and fathers of other countries where also grieving. How could I be happy that our missiles hit their targets; and, yet, I thanked God that they didn't hit my son. I believed in God's intervention because not only did I seem to be praying all the time, but I also had Kevin on countless prayer chains. We attended prayer vigils and special church services. I prayed that God would cover Kevin with "His blanket of protection" and bring him home safely.

I had said that I would not watch television constantly, but I ended up glued to that screen. I wanted to believe that I saw Kevin, and yet Cy reminded me that Kevin would likely not be in a place where he would be photographed. So, I would console myself that our country would do all they could to protect those serving in Intelligence not allowing myself to think about the fact that the enemy really wanted to wipe out our country's Intelligence installations.

We got through the days waiting for a letter or that coveted phone call. We were so relieved when it came. Brenda would let us know when she heard, and then our hope was renewed. But my questions about the wisdom of war plagued me. War brings suffering, and I have a hard time with the concept of a "just war." On the other hand, something has to be done about evil leaders.

The argument can be made that economic revival can come as a result of war. But is it worth it? I am not an expert on the subject; I am just a Mom who was thrilled when Desert Storm ended up being a short war. I chose to live in America, and I try to be patriotic by supporting our Military. As a former military Mom, a citizen of the United States and a Christian, I will continue to have questions. If enough people care and enough people question, maybe sometime there won't be so much weeping and grieving because of war.

Cy and I never discussed if we would go to North Carolina to Camp LeJuene to see Kevin come home. It was just an unspoken understanding between us that we would. We made plans to be able to leave within 24 hours or so after hearing from Brenda when Kevin would be on his way home. And that's what happened. We were there when he got off the bus; and along with his wife, we happily welcomed home a healthy young man whom we were extremely proud of. We spent a couple of days just getting to know him again and treasuring every moment of it.

A few years earlier we would never have imagined that our family would walk the path of war. But we did, and God was faithful. He walked with us just as He walked with those who struggled with the grief of losing their loved one. Just as we weep over the devastation that humanity brings upon itself, God weeps too. Never forget that no matter what path we either choose to take or are forced to take, He is not far from us. God's love is endless, and there is no limit to its boundaries. Wartime or peacetime – He walks with us.

dw

No Work Tomorrow

Five o'clock in the afternoon was a time I looked forward to because my husband, Cy, would soon be home from a long day's work. For 27 years he had been an Ironworker. When the children were young, we enjoyed occasional trips to downtown Minneapolis to see the buildings that Daddy had helped build. In the summer we would sometimes go to his job and have a picnic lunch with him and then stay and watch a while. We liked seeing the big equipment and the men climbing high in the air.

There wasn't much building construction going on in 1993 because the whole area was overbuilt. There were too many office buildings unoccupied. The Mall of America was finished; and, beside that, we were in the middle of a recession. Our oldest son, Brian, was in the Ironwork Apprenticeship Program; and he had recently been laid off his job too.

The real fear of a long layoff had been with us for a few months. But we consoled ourselves with the fact that Cy had been a company man for many years and chances were that they would do all they could to keep him employed. Even though the young son of the owner of the company he worked for had taken over, we hoped that he would certainly respect the experience of older workers.

The day had already turned to night as the bitter January cold persisted. I heard Cy's Jeep pull into our garage. When he came into the house, his first words were, "Well, I was laid off at the end of the day. I don't have a job to go to tomorrow."

"It'll just be for a week or two, won't it?" I asked anxiously.

"Probably not, there's just not much work out there."

For the first couple of weeks, Cy looked at the situation as a kind of vacation. He visited the library, puttered around the house and appreciated not working outside all day in the bitter cold weather. I continued to run my two home-based businesses. Before long, Cy started getting restless and began looking for jobs from friends and neighbors. He's blessed with a gift of being able to repair almost anything. Anything, that is, except the unemployment situation the building trades were experiencing.

After a few weeks I became anxious, and my mind went crazy with questions: How could we ever make it financially? Our daughter, Kimberly, was in college; how could we still help her? How much could we cut back? Would we use up all the reserves we had? I didn't have anymore hours in the day to take on any more sewing projects or to increase my direct sales business. The questions kept coming, and I panicked. We experienced a couple of weeks when both of us were edgy, argumentative and often at odds with each other. The financial pressure and anxiety were starting to get the best of us.

Cy had another interesting struggle. He kept putting off filing for unemployment. Maybe it had to do with denial or pride or just not wanting to admit that we needed the money.

"You've paid into unemployment all these years," I protested. "Go and file, we deserve it as well as anyone else does," I begged him.

Finally, he took that important step; and our panic subsided. We began to think of alternatives for Cy. He had always been an Ironworker, and he was close to 50 years old. It was almost inconceivable to think of changing his career at this point.

It was becoming evident from his conversations with other Ironworkers that many men who were almost 50 or over were in the same position as Cy. It was true that work was scarce, but it also seemed to be true that the new young boss didn't have much respect or appreciation for the seasoned worker.

"I may not work as fast as a 20 year old," Cy exclaimed, "but I think that I work a lot smarter."

We now had four basic facts to face: There was the recession; prior over-building meant that the need for commercial buildings had dramatically decreased; the new boss had a bad attitude toward older workers; and when and if Cy went back to work, it would likely have to be with another company.

I experienced more anger over the situation than Cy did. I wanted to take that young punk of a boss by the shirt collar and rattle his teeth a little. I wanted to verbally list for him all the times in the past when

Cy's expertise had made money for the company. I wanted to remind him of how his Dad had appreciated Cy. I wanted "this kid" to shape up and change the situation.

Cy was a bit more realistic. He was disgusted with the situation but was unwilling to spend the energy on being angry and upset. "This is the way the new boss is and nothing will change him," was his attitude.

As weeks melted into months, Cy started picking up work in the neighborhood. He was willing to do anything from changing the light bulbs for the elderly to putting new shingles on a friend's roof. Some jobs were big enough that he was glad he could call on Brian for some help. It wasn't steady work, but every job was really appreciated.

I became aware of the plight of other unemployed people. I also knew that even if the worst should ever happen and we couldn't continue to live in our present home, all that really mattered was that we were together. We would live in our travel trailer in Wisconsin if we had to. We could downsize and cut corners, and I knew with all certainty that between the two of us, we wouldn't end up on the street. God had blessed us with 26 years of marriage, and we had obtained quite a few assets. We had a long way to go before ending up on the street. I regained my trust that God would supply our needs. The emphasis was on needs not necessarily wants. I reminded myself that God cared about this situation too and would see us through.

Summer came and we enjoyed more freedom. I found that I was especially enjoying the freedom of not worrying about him on his dangerous job. We were praying, however, for some ironwork to come his way – maybe even six months a year for the next six years until he could retire. That would provide us with health insurance coverage. Although it was more important than ever to put a lot of time in my Shaklee and Sewing businesses, we did have more together time. Because I saw more of him, I became more aware of the gifts God had given Cy. Oh yes, there were still plenty of frustrations centered mainly around the adjustment of not really knowing our weekly income.

A frustration for Cy was not having a "place" in the world of employment. Part of our identity is our job. When someone asks,

"What do you do for a living?" you know how to reply without hesitation. Cy struggled about how to answer that question. With the loss of employment, comes the loss of financial security that he had provided all these years. At times that was manifested in loss of self-esteem and some depression.   Although he seemed to get lots of odd jobs, the pay was very minimal. Usually a person's wage gives a sense of worth. When your place on the pay scale lowers dramatically, there are still more adjustments to be made. We had to ask ourselves just how important that "place" was.

Eventually, another company talked with Cy and said they could give him work for four months, until January of 1994. We were thankful for the job. But now I was have many conflicting emotions. I actually cried, because it meant he would be gone every day all day long again. I had grown to really like our together-lifestyle, and part of me didn't want to see that change.

He worked those four months, and then the same company asked if he would work for a couple of months on another job. Things seemed to be looking up financially at least. Soon after that job was done, he actually was hired back by his old company. This was after he made many calls and finally talked with a new man who was now dispatching the workers. Of course we had no idea how long this would last.

I began to realize that I had learned many lessons through this experience. I started counting my blessings in new ways. We didn't plan on the much-needed vacation because of too much uncertainty with his employment. However, we did spend as many weekends as possible at our Wisconsin land. If we ate out, it was only the inexpensive places that got our money. We recycled and re-used more than we ever had.

Loss of employment encompasses a grieving process and then a time to reflect and find another place in life. We prayed a lot; friends were supportive and caring and WE DIDN'T GIVE UP. We were, after all, not the only ones in this situation. We learned how to make changes in our life as they were needed.

When Cy went back to work, I missed him like I had not before. We had found a new appreciation for each other and a new enjoyment of being together. We now could really look forward to retirement and spending much more time together.

After working for a few different contractors, Cy was offered the opportunity to start his own company. This particular contractor would provide the start-up money, and Cy and Brian would incorporate. This did happen, and now we totally own "Erector's Inc." God had been working in this situation too and bringing new opportunities. They had done a job that was featured in a national magazine that, consequently, had a lot to do with getting the attention of the right people.

Brian now has a real pride in his company and his work. It has worked wonders for him in his life. God has given father and son the ability to work together. Chances are things would not have worked out this way if the layoff had not occurred.

So there are often times when we experience loss of our "place" in life. Walking through that experience may be very difficult. The path takes twists and turns and at times seems very uncertain. But God knows where we are. He knows what our needs are and he knows what is best for us. Eventually, we can look back and see that the place we are in now is even better than the place we came from.

dw

Following is the account of my friend Phyllis' journey with her husband during his last year of life. We will follow her as she made crucial decisions and cared for him. I was deeply touched by her strong faith as she walked this road.

Tea and the Holy Spirit

This morning the sun is low on the horizon.
The burdens of the day seem very heavy.
My friend, Phyllis, sits at her kitchen table alone.
She is without her husband, Bill, of almost 35 years.
He is a patient at a nursing home for a time
as he fights for his life as a result of diabetes.
A recent stroke has now clouded his mind.
She has already lost him in so many ways.

There are many important decisions to be made.
"Phyllis," I asked when I called her, "How are you today?"
She calmly replied, "I'm just sitting here in the kitchen
sipping tea and drinking in the Holy Spirit."
Her answer has been forever imprinted on my heart.

Bill had been diagnosed with diabetes many years earlier.
In 1993 his symptoms had begun to worsen.
On a trip to Cancun, he needed much more rest than usual.
Then his kidneys began to fail and dialysis became necessary.
But Bill's determination won, and he learned how to
accept the responsibility of doing dialysis at home.
Dialysis was a very frightening thing for Phyllis.
She knew that his health was deteriorating rapidly.
This illness had become a nightmare for her.

August 1994 resulted in a heart bypass for Bill.
Then in September he suffered the first stroke.

He was left confused, unable to read or finish a thought.
But that wasn't all – because of a foot infection
October brought an amputation above the ankle.
That is when nursing home care became necessary.
Physical therapy was attempted to prepare for a prosthesis.
Bill's brain just couldn't function well enough to continue.

Day upon day and month upon month
the horror of Bill's illness brought loss of hope -
hope for improvement and loss of hope for the future.
The grief over his suffering was overwhelming!
Then there was the worry over dwindling finances.
She could always trust Bill to stretch the money to pay bills.
Her challenge was to appear calm for their 16 year-old daughter.
Phyllis needed to insure her daughter's future with or without her loving daddy.

One December day as Phyllis prayed for strength and guidance,
She opened her daily reading to "Beware of Practical Atheism."
She proceeded to tell me the impact of the reading that day.
"This reading opened my consciousness to the possibility of a miracle.
I became aware that a miracle could mean many things.
I realized that my praying had been shallow at times -
not fully trusting in God, possibly my motto being,
'God helps those who help themselves.'
At that point I started watching for possible miracles.
I had a new faith that God had a plan for us -
that He loved us and wouldn't leave us floundering.
I could feel His Everlasting Arms enfold us
through all the people who where around supporting us.
It was the worst of times and the best of times."

She clung to this new trust as she grieved for her husband.
Bill was getting worse and could not converse.
Yet, he often seemed to know what was going on.
He would say to her, "Home, now, let's go."

The time had come for the most crucial decision of all.
If Bill did go home, dialysis would need to be discontinued.
His quality of life was gone, and the comfort of home may be best.
Maybe he would live longer than the doctor said, she hoped.
Bill wanted to come home; she was sure of it.

The doctor encouraged Phyllis to talk to Bill about it.
So she did just that – being sure that he understood what it meant.
She was feeling half-numb when she sat with him.
Bill plainly said to her, "Let's go for it, Phyl."
The decision was made, and Hospice became involved.
Within a day, a bed and other items were moved into their home.

Bill was now at home where he desperately wanted to be.
Their six children became even more involved in his care.
Neighbors and friends brought food and offered to help.
Many times the family would pray with their visitors.
The one or two weeks that they were told he could live
without dialysis had now become almost three weeks.
One day Bill asked his daughter to take him to his
favorite fancy grocery store which was near their home.
With the help of a wheelchair, they went on his last adventure.

A few days later while Phyllis rubbed Bill's back, she assured him that
he had been a good husband and father; and they could make it.
They moved him to his favorite chair placing his feet on a footstool.
The assurance that Phyllis had given him seemed to release him.
He closed his eyes, and they soon realized that he had peacefully
and so very quietly given up the fight and passed from this life.

I asked Phyllis for some reflections on that time in her life.
She said that Bill had always bounced back from a setback.
So after the stroke she didn't expect it to be the beginning of the end.
It was when he couldn't read and would at times become confused
that she began to realize she was actually losing him.

She is now happy that they did bring him home for his last days.
Sometime after Bill's death, I asked Phyllis
what the hardest thing was about not having him there.
She thoughtfully replied that it was so hard and so lonely
to not have him to talk with about decisions that had to be made.
Bill had put up shelves in the den to display some of his things.
Now several years later those shelves and his things are still there.

Phyllis' life has become one of easy communication with God.
"It's kind of just talking with him throughout the day," she explained.
She told me that the time she spent in her prayer chair
was extremely important to her then, and still is now.
"Ever since that reading of December 7, 1994
I've had an awakening and a renewed faith in God.
I know and I trust that He will not let me down.
In God's own time He will work for my greater good.
Through prayer and through patience, all will be well."

"Do you prayer walk?" she asked me. I asked her what she meant.
"It's praying for each person in the four beat rhythm of your steps.
Deeply breathe in the Holy Spirit and breathe out the negative
thoughts."
With those words I was sweetly reminded once again –
"I am just sitting here sipping tea and drinking in the Holy Spirit."

dw

Beware of Practical Atheism
Wednesday, December 7 · Second Week of Advent

They that hope in the Lord will renew their strength, they
will soar as with eagles' wings. Isaiah 40:31

How many miracles have you experienced in your personal life? None? That is only because you weren't expecting any. God never lets you down when your expectations of him are high; he may keep you waiting, or he may come at once, or he may come suddenly and unexpectedly like a "thief in the night," to use Jesus' expression. But he surely will if you are expecting him to come.

Someone has said that *the* sin against the Holy Spirit is to no longer believe that he can change the world, to no longer believe that he can change me. This is a more dangerous kind of atheist than those who say, "God does not exist," for, while telling themselves they believe in God, they have blinded themselves into a practical atheism of which they are hardly aware…. The God of these people is, for all practical purposes, a dead God—not the God who by raising Jesus from the dead has shown us that nothing is impossible to him.

God, help me to hope in you grace so that I may be renewed in spirit.

Fr. Anthony de Mello, S.J.
Contact With God

Is 40:25-31 · Ps 103 · Mt 11:28-30

ChapterFour

TheJourney OfRaising OurChildren

Children are God's gift to our present and our future. They are the most fragile of all gifts – handle with care, love and prayer.

Just By Being Here

Just by being here -
You have a place in God's world.
It may seem to be small -
of no significance at all.
But make no mistake, dear child,
by being here, you are important to God.

Just by being here -
There is something special for you to do.
You may not be president of anything,
but you are good at something.
So, don't feel unneeded or useless -
you do have a reason and a purpose.

Just by being here -
You are a totally unique individual.
You are truly different from anyone.
Your mind and heart is yours alone.
So find that something special to give
to the glory of God and begin to really live!

dw

Train Up a Child

"Train up a child in the way he should go; and when he is old, he will not turn from it." *Proverbs 22:6*

It is amazing to me how God, in His Word, has in some way addressed every problem we may encounter in life. He must have known that raising children could be a real challenge when they are feeling their independence and doing all they can to experience as much as possible of what the world has to offer. Today, in our culture these experiences can be exciting and healthy contributing to their growth into well-rounded adults. However, there is the other side of the coin. There is so much that is unhealthy, so much that is detrimental to their growth, and so much that is downright dangerous. Sometimes it is really scary for parents to let their children go on their own meeting friends and making decisions about how they will live their lives.

We used to think that the only kids who messed up their lives were those who had come from bad neighborhoods or from what was called dysfunctional homes. The term dysfunctional isn't used as much anymore, maybe because it is too broad. Unless we are perfect people living in perfect families, there is likely something that could be termed as dysfunctional within every family. We thought that children who struggled with identity must have come from broken homes or homes where one of the parents was probably suffering from substance abuse. We thought that kids who always had to do things the hard way or take the long road in learning life's lessons certainly must have come from a home without proper discipline and guidance. If a teenager got into trouble with the law, it was usually so embarrassing for the parents that the child may have been kicked out of the house. Our own judgment might include something like, "If only they had attended church and Sunday school every week and lived in a Christian home, things would have been different for them." The interesting and sad thing is that even children brought up in Christian homes may sometimes go their own way for a time to experiment with or take part in the not-so-healthy things the world has to offer. The challenge of raising emotionally, physically and spiritually healthy children crosses all lines of race and economic status. I think we have the picture.

It seems that families have had troubles from the very beginning. I would imagine that Adam and Eve were devastated when Cain killed his brother Abel out of jealousy. "How could he have done such a thing?" they must have asked. Then there were Isaac and Rebekah's sons, Esau and Jacob who were twins. In this case Mom, Rebekah, and Dad, Isaac, each had their favorites; and it was a family of deception vying for the birthright. Talk about a dysfunctional family; that certainly was one. Don't forget Jacob and Rachel with their 12 sons. Joseph was second to the youngest and was his father's favorite son, which made the other 11 sons very jealous. They certainly schemed and carried out their plan to "get rid of Joseph." Obviously, trouble with children started at the beginning when sin entered this world. In some ways things haven't changed all that much from the creation of the human race. However, we are more aware than ever that just because we do all we can to raise our children with Christian values, provide a loving home, bring them to instruction in the Faith, and to church on the Lord's Day, we are not guaranteed that their "growing into adult years" will be without its frustrations and troubles. In fact, many such families are experiencing numerous challenges raising their teenagers.

It is every newly married couple's dream that everything will go smoothly throughout their entire life. They will become successful, raise wonderful children who will also become successful. The fact is that we do wake up from that dream and life happens. When those crises come (and they will), when they are personal, when they are ours to handle, where does our strength come from?

Our family wasn't exempt from teenage trials. Our one son just seemed to have to take the long way around everything. My husband and I were often at odds with how to handle discipline situations in those teen years. Cy was much stricter than I. On reflection, I should not have second-guessed him as often as I did. I, on the other hand, liked to talk things through. Thinking that reason would prevail is sometimes expecting a lot when dealing with teens because their reasoning is immature and doesn't include how their decisions can impact their future. Oh yes, I did my share of raising my voice and grounding, but I think I was afraid of losing. Not losing the battle over the issue at the time, but of losing my child altogether. You see, we had sheltered several teenagers overnight because they had been kicked out of their own home. One actually stayed a few months. I absolutely believed that one thing I would never do was to lock the door on my kids. The situation would have to be so bad and extremely dangerous for the rest of the family before I would even consider something so drastic as locking out my own child. I thank God that we never had to consider "throwing the kid out."

I do know what it was like to get a call because a child was picked up for a DWI. I was glad that he was caught before causing an accident and hurting someone. But I couldn't understand how he could be so stupid. I was embarrassed and angry. Alcohol and drugs were easy to get and were being used a lot by high school kids in the late 80's. Even the kids from the well-to-do families were using them; they had more money, and it was the "in" thing. Our children went to what was considered a good inner suburban school. But that didn't matter; substance abuse in the "80's was rampant.

Then there was the second DWI. It was absolutely devastating for us. This time he lost his drivers license. What would we do with this teenager? He always had jobs; he didn't drop out of school; he went with us to church; and he was usually considerate of us when at home. But he was messing up. I cried and I prayed. When they are this age, it is impossible to keep them at home at all times; and if he wasn't driving, he had lots of friends who were. I was embarrassed, and I really did feel like I was failing as a mother, and we were failing as parents.

It was then that I really embraced the verse from *Proverbs 22:6*, "Train up a child in the way in which he should go, and when he is old he will not turn from it." My interpretation of that verse is that it is a directive, a guide or maybe even a command from our wise God. The words after the "and" are as a promise – "when he is old, he will not turn from it." This is certainly to be interpreted without gender in mind. What a promise it is! These 10 words hold great and wonderful hope to parents concerned about their children. It seems to say that the child will return as the prodigal son did in *Luke chapter 15. In Isaiah 55:11* we read, "So is my word that goes out from my mouth; it shall not return to me empty, but it will accomplish that I desire and achieve the purpose for which I sent it." If we are faithful parents who have taught God's Word in our home and have brought our children to our place of Worship for nourishment and instruction so they have heard God's Word, we can trust that Scripture. That, too, is a promise. A promise from God regarding what He will do. His word will not be for nothing, but will be for His glory. We parents need to be in The Word; need to be studying and praying and holding on to these wonderful promises. Then we will be strong enough to love our children through anything and never give up hope. *I Timothy 1:5 RSV* reads, "...whereas the aim of our charge is love that issues from a pure heart and a good conscience and sincere faith." We are to love our children and our spouse. Just love, and love and love.

We usually kept most of these troubles within our home because it was too hard to talk about. We would try to deal with it on our own. If I had to do it over, I wouldn't do that. I would at least share with a good friend, or seek counseling. At least the kids didn't run away. I made it a point to know the names and addresses of their friends; and much to their embarrassment, I would call and check on them and sometimes even show up at the door. In our society when so many things are accepted behavior and our young people have access to so much, both good and bad, parents really don't have a lot of control once the kids reach their mid-teens. We have to do all we can to know where they are going and whom they are going to be with. You know, even good kids make bad decisions sometimes. The scary thing is that at this age the bad decision can sometimes have long-term consequences.

I asked God every day that He would send guardian angels to watch over my family. They worked over-time, I am sure. At times the best teacher was consequences for their actions by some one other than Mom and Dad.

High School graduation day finally came. Our dear son had actually made it, and we were so proud and relieved. He was working and had a girlfriend. Then came another mistake – an early marriage that ended after a year. The decision to end that marriage was not a mistake. Within a year or so he began apprenticeship school and followed in his Dad's footsteps by becoming a very good Ironworker.

The time came when we did seek counseling for our other son who was having a real identity problem. He is adopted, and teen years were not always easy for him either. He is of mixed race and didn't always know where or how to fit in. He was very intelligent and such a deep thinker but wasn't working up to his potential in high school. We had some confrontations with a couple of his teachers, which is our responsibility as parents. He joined an anti-racist group during high school – one that did give us some concern. However, it didn't seem to do him any harm. We do really have to be careful what kinds of groups our children get involved with. This time, however, going to counseling was a good thing for him as well as for us. This is the son who became a Marine after graduation and was trained for and served in Military Intelligence.

You are now probably saying to yourself, "Since my child has messed up so much, and has lied to me, how can I ever trust him/her again?" That is really tough. You've probably heard, "Don't you trust me anymore?" To be honest you may have to just say, "No, I really don't." Regaining trust is a long hard road. If anyone has betrayed our trust in any way, our relationship with that person has changed. When it is our child and we feel responsible for their actions, it is sheer agony when some degree or all trust is gone. The person has to know that their actions and their actions only will help us to regain trust in them. For a child that means respecting and obeying the rules that the parents have set for their home. It means doing a better job at school and, of course, always attending. It means realizing when they've violated that trust again and taking responsibility for it. If these things are done, trust will be established again slowly but surely. It takes patience. It's wonderful when that relationship is restored.

I am convinced that even when a child is making bad choices, it is most important to underscore something special about him/her. If there is a feeling of, " it doesn't matter anyway because I can't do anything right," the chances of the child changing is more remote. We all need assurance that we are good at something and are appreciated, giving us a needed boost in our self-image. A teacher once told me to be sure to say something good or compliment my children every day. Sometimes you may have to search for that something; but no matter how small the complement, it can work wonders. I was also reminded that our children usually make more good decisions than bad ones.

I wish I had been better at picking my battles. Maybe haircuts or lack of and weird styles of dress aren't really important in the end. There are certainly many important issues that really do have to be addressed; so it isn't always worth it to create a war over less important issues that aren't going to be harmful to the child or anyone else. Often it's our image we are more concerned about. What will my friends think about that haircut, those baggy pants, or the shirt tied around the waist? Being realistic with curfews and learning to compromise on some issues can keep the peace in the home. If we are always ragging on them for non-important matters, home isn't going to be a nice place to be. It is so important that our children look at home as an escape from peer pressure and other frustrations and a place they want to be. It is also the best way to keep kids from running away from home.

You may be reading this and wondering how in the world to survive some situations with your children. I'm not an expert, I am just a Mom who raised three teenagers. But we never gave up believing that God had great plans for our kids. Now many years later, they are wonderful adults, successful and growing in their relationships with God. We are so thankful for that.

I remember that after the boys had left home, I had asked God for some positive signs that they were OK. One day we received a call from California where our oldest son was working. He proceeded to say, "Mom and Dad I just called to say that I am so sorry for what I have put you through. The way you have worried and the way I have messed up." We could tell he was crying. What a gift he gave us with that telephone call. Our other son called one time and thanked us for sticking with him and never giving up on him. We thanked God for those wonderful and encouraging words.

In the end all we can really do is our best and remember that none of us is perfect. Our children aren't perfect, and we aren't perfect parents. There isn't practice or a dry run for the most important job in the world – the job of parenting. Remember our aim is to love, to rely on God's promises, and to trust that in everything God works for the good.

For those of you who are reading this and are in the midst of the Deep Woods because your prodigal has not returned, keep the vigil. Pray always and never give up. Where there is life there is always hope. If you don't even know where your child is, remember that God does; and there is no territory for His guardian angels. So your prayers of protection and a change of heart for your child can yield great results. Never, never weary in praying for your child. If that child does not return in your lifetime, which I think would be the worst, be assured that his or her life may have positive effects on someone else – never cease hoping. If the results for your child have been tragic or even if their life was lost, only God's strength, and His alone, can keep you. It will not fail you and will bring you through the Deep Woods where you must walk. You will then be on that journey that others, who have seen their children die, are on. You can, however, be assured that God is there with you. We can trust that through God's unfailing love and grace there will be light in your life again.

dw

Rooted and Grounded

In the book of *Ephesians Chapter 3 verses 14-21NRSV* we find a prayer that Paul prayed for his congregation in Ephesus while he was in prison in Rome. I have found this prayer helpful to personalize and pray for each of my children individually or for our family. This is the prayer -

For this reason, I come before you dear Father, from whom every family in heaven and on earth takes its name. I pray that, according to the riches of your glory, you may grant my children to be strengthened in their inner being with power through your Spirit, and that Christ may dwell in their hearts through faith, as they are being rooted and grounded in love. I pray that they may have the power to comprehend, with all the saints, what is the breadth and length and height and depth, and to know the love of Christ that surpasses knowledge, so that they may be filled with all the fullness of God.

Now to you, Father, who by the power at work within us is able to accomplish abundantly far more than all we can ask or imagine, to you be glory in the church and in Christ Jesus to all generations, forever and ever. Amen.

dw

The Family Broken and Healed

Webster defines "family" in the traditional sense of mother, father, brothers and sisters. It also defines family as a group of related or similar things, or a group of individuals who are not necessarily related.

Under any definition, family is belonging. The sad reality is that many members of families no longer feel as though they belong, and the family becomes broken. I was shocked by how many friends my children had when they were in school who came from broken families.

Even within the traditional family style much brokeness can occur. When a family member has become troubled or is in trouble, it affects everyone else in the family. When one member suffers; all members suffer.

Often anger takes over. "We didn't raise you that way," a parent shouts, or "How could you have done that?!" Then blaming and tears follow.

It is not always easy to love. In fact, sometimes it is extremely exhausting and downright painful. There are times when nights are spent tossing and turning while you are attempting to turn off the movie that keeps playing over and over in your mind. Peace and rest seem totally out of reach.

Hopefully, through the heartache, we will know that somehow we will survive if only we can stick together as a family. We all make mistakes, even though some are much more serious than others are. If one family member has made decisions that hurt and exclude the rest of the family, he or she needs to know that the doors are open and forgiveness is waiting. If we stick together, there will be support, love and a refuge. We must guard against the family becoming so fragile that it will shatter like Humpty Dumpty never to be put together again.

Anger, hurt and disappointment can be overwhelming. As our children grow, disappointment is probably the hardest to deal with. Often keeping the family together means letting go to allow a child to develop and to become the unique individual God meant him or her to be. Let mistakes be made, they can be wonderful learning experiences. Allowing the individual to rectify the mistakes may be hard to do, but it is the most important action of all. If it results in embarrassment or suffering, we need to have patience for the process.

We shouldn't try to make our children clones of ourselves. The beauty of family is the diversity of its members. We don't think the same or feel the same or deal in the same way with life. Some of our families are even more diverse because we have adopted children from other cultures. Sometimes families don't have the same skin color. These and other differences can make a beautiful mosaic in the family.

This family mosaic demands much communication and acceptance. Acceptance means loving each person for who he or she is and respecting where they are in their life at the present moment. Acceptance does not mean giving up on our own morals or beliefs. I believe that God comes to us where we are. Can we do less for one another?

Here comes the "however" – we do have a responsibility to each other. We need to be keenly aware that we can cause other family members to suffer because of our actions or our words. There certainly is some value in not being caught up in what other's think. Yet, we DO NOT live in a vacuum. We DO live in a community. How society pictures us may very well be important for our practical every day living. Teens often want to be left alone to dress and look and act in any way they desire; "it's just no one else's business." Guess again! It can for various reasons affect other members of the family. Sadly, teens often don't think beyond themselves and their friends. They don't realize the distress and suffering their actions can cause. Only we parents know how we can start blaming ourselves when our kids mess up, asking how we could have been better parents. Their actions can have ripple effects that may be very difficult to deal with.

Preteens and teens often don't think about future consequences of doing what they want when they want. They need to be confronted with the negative sides of what their actions are or could bring to themselves and others. Ask them if it is really worth it stressing that they will be held responsible for their actions.

The family unit can better weather all kinds of storms and face all types of calamities, surviving every possible disaster, if we join hands and stand united. We are loyal to one another, and we give love and support when it is needed. Someone is always handy to give a hug and dry the tears. Even when there is sadness and difficulties, we are solid and secure. No one under any circumstance can break the family bond!!

Wouldn't that scenario be wonderful? The sad fact is that life happens and brokeness occurs. The world may at times seem cold and without justice. We may look for hope but only feel frustrated and alone. We bring our children up to be independent; and when they exhibit that independence, we recoil and wish that they were back in the safety of the nest. So, what do we do?

Let's concentrate on that family unit. Sometimes staying together is work – hard work; but it also has its rewards. There may be the necessity of family and individual counseling. Trust may have to be earned again and certainly forgiveness needs to take place along with restored or improved communication. By God's grace a family can survive in spite of brokeness, and healing can come. We may not agree with one another, but we can accept that. We can learn to pick our battles, to compromise and respect one another.

There will be times when anger occurs. It is important that it isn't the "wish-I-could-take-it-back" outburst that is hurtful or bitter. We must continue the struggle of letting go at the appropriate time to allow our children to grow. At times we'll feel like we are groping through a maze to find peace; but if we stay together, there will always be someone for us. Our hearts and our doors will remain open to one another. It isn't magic; it is rooted deep in love. However, when the wink of approval and "that was very nice, Mom," or "I love you" hugs are shared, the work is worth everything you went through.

When the tunnel is long and light doesn't seem to appear, don't give up hope. God's love never fails, God can and still is actively working in the world and often in mysterious ways. So, pray and believe, and let God help your family walk together as a healthy, strong unit.

Remember Timothy tells us "Whereas the aim of our charge is love that issues from a pure heart and a good conscience and sincere faith, " *I Timothy 1:5 RSV.*

It Takes a Village*

It takes a whole Village to raise children today.
People to nurture, love and show them the way.
Parents, grandparents, Godparents, aunts and uncles too,
Plus cousins, friends and the neighbor next door,
Sunday School teachers and Pastors are a part of the crew,
As well as school teachers, doctors, nurses and many more.

All are a part of a very important community
With the world's most important job to do.
To guide and direct this child of God, you see;
Takes wisdom, patience, love and a special part of you.

So with faith and hope encompassed by prayer
All must join hands and always be there.
For one day, this child, a part of the village will be
That is nurturing and raising their own family.

dw

*The title, *It Takes a Village to Raise a Child* is an African Proverb.

A dear friend whom I love like a sister contributed the following story. She and her husband, like many other parents, experienced their teenager having a child before marriage. Her story is not unique, except it is always unique when it is being experienced personally. Maybe you are facing this same situation right now. Maybe her story will give you the encouragement you need to keep right on loving and right on hanging in there with your child. You will experience her faith shinning through her words.

Premature Grandma
By Vickie Johnson

It's planting time; and I'm reminded of the year that I planted potatoes, but the harvest produced salty potato chips. *Matthew 5:13* says, "You are the salt of the earth...." Well, I was doing my part! Really, I was often crying when I was hoeing the potatoes; it does not take a lot of concentration to get the weeds out. It does, however, take a lot of prayer and God's help to deal with the challenges of life.

In today's world there are many different family arrangements. The typical family of two people growing up, marrying, having children and staying together until one dies is no longer as common. Well, back in the forties when my husband and I were born, we both entered into an unusual family experience. My husband's mother died when he was six weeks old. He had five older brothers ranging in age from ten to eighteen. My husband's father gave him to a couple who only had one child, and then they moved two states away. I was born six months after my dad died in the Normandy Invasion of World War II. My mother and I then lived with her parents. Both my husband and I were raised in Christian homes where we were loved and taught to live lives honoring God and our fellow human beings.

The Bible has many verses that speak about God supplying us with strength. Our typical family of three children was going to face a tremendous challenge. Our teen-age daughter became pregnant when she was still in high school. *Psalm 30:5 RSV* talks about crying in the night but joy comes in the morning. It took longer than that! That's when the potatoes got salted; but, also, prayers were raised.

Our family and friends gave support and encouragement, and God was at work, too.

Romans 8:28 RSV says, "We know that in everything God works for good with those who love him." What "good" was there? We received a beautiful grandchild and got to enjoy him every day. We saw our daughter take full responsibility for her child, graduate from high school, and from junior college. We are proud of her for the love, character, and strength that she shows in all areas in her life. We now can say, 'Rejoice always, pray constantly, give thanks in all circumstances; for this is the will of God in Christ Jesus for you." *I Thessalonians 5:16-18 RSV*

dw

Marked Forever

I know a fine young man in his thirties who has several tattoos. In his young adult years he went through a time of searching – searching for a career, for excitement, his own identity, and wanting to be in control of his own life. His friends were not the best for positively influencing his decisions. In fact, sometimes quite the opposite was true. At that time in his life, he got a tattoo. Then his friend, who was quite a good artist, started a little side business of tattooing. So this young man got another one and another one. I'm really not sure how many he now has.

Tattoos are pretty permanent on your body. Now years later he admits that there are times when he wishes that he had not gotten so many, and there is one that he regrets. However, it doesn't do any good to think about it now. What's done is done.

This young man now has his life together, has a career and is growing in his relationship with his God. However, his body is marked forever because of the decision made in his youth.

His mother has said that the tattoos bother her and make her sad. However, she can now look beyond them to the fine person that he is and appreciate his wonderful heart. She is glad that he didn't go along with the current fads of piercing his nose or tongue.

This man's body is marked and only lots of money and many procedures can change that. Most parents forgive their children when they do foolish things that bring them distress. Something so visible is hard to forget, but it can be overlooked. Just as when we come to God asking for forgiveness, He also forgives us. God overlooks our dumb mistakes and even our horrendous sins once they have been given to Him.

At Baptism we are marked forever with the Cross of Christ. Jesus Christ took all our sins and regrets with Him to that cross where they died with him. With that comes the freedom of living life to its fullest in the way God intends us to. No matter what marks our past may have given us – our future has been bought by Christ and is secure in the Hands of our Heavenly Father.

dw

Patience for the Process

We seem to live in a world that goes faster every day. We have instant food, instant access to the world via television and the internet, and jets that get us to our destination in record time. We are always hurrying to get it done or to go somewhere.

In this society the whole concept of patience can be lost. We don't have the time to wait at ramp meter lights, for the car ahead of us to make its turn, for a slow computer to connect, or a long line at the checkout counter. Yet, patience is not only a requirement for getting along with other people in life, it is the one thing that can yield great rewards of achievements well done. Patience is a virtue that heals; it waits while growing and maturing happens. We plant a seed and wait for the flower; it will grow only as fast as the conditions surrounding that flower and the care it is given will allow it to grow. Only then can we enjoy its beauty and take pride in a job done well.

The most important job or career in this world is that of raising our children. If you are a parent, there is no other job more important than bringing your children up to be emotionally, physically and spiritually healthy. That takes patience while the lessons of life are learned.

When our children were little, we may have been surprised by the so-called terrible two's and toddler tantrums. We soon found ourselves being anxious for them to be old enough to go to school. The day came, and we couldn't believe where the time had gone. When they were old enough to help with chores, we probably urged them to hurry up and do them; and "please, do a good job." Then the teen years were upon us, and we found ourselves talking a different language than they did, and we longed for the time when they would finally find themselves and settle down.

The time flew by, and we found ourselves struggling to remember all the cute things they did and special times we had; and only then realizing that we had wished away a lot of the time. It takes a flower time to grow and mature into beautiful blooms. It takes a life many years to grow and learn and develop its own personality and mature into an adult. That journey, however, can be one of excitement, joy and great delight. Patience is needed to aid that process and for relationships to develop and grow with love. God knows how we can best serve Him with our life. What a privilege to be a part of helping our children find that purpose for their lives so they will be well equipped for their journey. Best of all, we will have taught them that they will never be alone because they can hold their Heavenly Father's hand all the way.

dw

Chapter Five

Our Daily Walk

"This is the day which the Lord has made;
let us rejoice and be glad in it." Psalm 118:24

War and Bedspreads

In a sense I guess I was born into a "Deep Woods" because World War II was underway. I don't remember a lot about it because I was so young. I do remember a few things, however; or, I remember being told them. Mom was always concerned about our supply of sugar because of rationing. There wasn't much money for many years after the war either. Often we ate oatmeal for breakfast, and my mother made the leftovers into fried patties, and served them with homemade maple syrup for supper. We had lots of dairy products and meat products from the farm. Mom also gardened and canned in the summer, so we were never without food. But there were very lean years – years of saving flowered flour sacks to use for sewing dresses and curtains and many other items. I can't say that we suffered, we just had never experienced anything better. The bitter winter cold meant piling on more quilts and firing up the wood furnace more often. We walked a lot more then; because there were no school buses. But we were a family, and we belonged to a community that watched out for and cared for each other. We also were a part of a wonderful Christian family at our little country church.

When I was much older, I learned something about those war years that impacted me in a powerful way. I was given a beautifully crocheted bedspread. My grandmother, my father's mother, had laboriously made it and several others during the war. You see, four of their eight children were all serving in the war at the same time. Two of her daughters were nurses and their twin sons were also serving (one as a fighter pilot).

Wow! I can only begin to imagine how she must have been holding her Father's Hand so tightly during that time. We had a son who served in the Gulf War. It was one of the deepest woods I have ever been in. We waited daily for a phone call or a letter in the mail and were elated when either happened. During World War II, communications were much slower. Telephones weren't always available and the mail took much longer to be delivered. My father's parents had four children to give to the Lord every day who needed His loving protection. Our family was very blessed that they all returned safely.

Grandma had a talent – she could crochet beautifully. So, she kept her mind and her hands busy as she made bedspreads. The one I have was made out of grocery string, and only God knows how many prayers are woven into the beautiful designs that she created in each and every bedspread that she made. There may have even been a tear or many tears that fell as she thought of her children being in danger and not knowing how they were. But she continued creating something warm and beautiful with every movement of her fingers. My grandmother was a woman of faith, and she walked through that Deep Woods to the sunlight when her children came home once again. Now several of us are blessed to have a bedspread to remind us of our grandmother's journey.

dw

My Grandmother's Bedspread

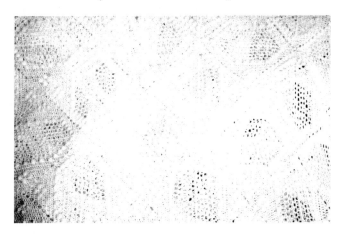

For I Am Convinced

"For I am convinced that neither death, nor life, nor angels, nor rulers, nor things present, nor things to come, nor powers, nor height, nor depth, nor anything else in all creation will be able to separate us from the love of God in Christ Jesus our lord." *Romans 8:38-39 NRSV*

Dear God, thank you for these words of promise to us. Just knowing that nothing, absolutely nothing can separate me from your love is all I need for today and for tomorrow and for always. I am convinced, as the Apostle Paul was, that your love manifested in your Son, Christ Jesus our Lord, is all I need to never be alone and all I need for all eternity. Amen.

dw

Linda is my sister-in-law. By sitting and listening and talking with her, I have learned much about what it is like to come from the place of not knowing Jesus to truly trusting in Him. She is married to my husband's brother, Bill. I treasure the fellowship in Christ that we now have. These are Linda's words as she shared them with me.

My Walk to Trusting Jesus
Linda's Story

The biggest stumbling blocks to my becoming a Christian were people who said that they were "good Christian people." They say they are, but they don't live it. These people know scripture; it doesn't matter how they interpret it, but they know it. Consequently, they trip up people who are searching. I know why people never come to Christ. They run into too many walls. You know, you have to feel Jesus in your heart. You have no idea what someone feels like when they are searching, when they are down in the pits. I wish I could have seen the light suddenly, like Saul on the road to Damascus; I wish I could have had that experience. But I didn't – it was a long road for me. If only "good Christians" would know how they can be stumbling blocks. As human beings, we can all get off on the wrong track, but God still loves us.

My husband, Bill, and I used to laugh at a Christian friend because she would say, "Praise the Lord" for everything. She would find a parking place and she would say, "Praise the Lord!" But now I know how she was feeling. To try to put into words how I got to this place with God is difficult. I went to a Cursillos weekend. It is a time dedicated to how much God really loves you.

Let me tell you about the first time that I went some place with Bill. It was to Wednesday night Lenten Services.

He said, " Come to church with me tonight, please."

I replied, "You know I'm just not very interested in church. The people there are not receptive."

He pleaded, " Just come with me; it will make me feel good."

So, I went, and the service was about loving divorced people. I asked Bill if he knew that's what the sermon was going to be about.

He said, "No, that's the Lord at work."

"Yeah sure," I thought. But I remember that whole service. I think that my divorce was the worst thing that ever happened to me because we are supposed to honor our marriage vows. It was the shame and feeling of failure, and it is still hard to talk about. I still have those feelings.

The Cursillos weekend was where I said, "Yes" to Jesus. It was an experience that I can't begin to explain to you. Bill was persistent that I attend. The husband goes the first weekend, and the wife goes the second weekend. Jody's wedding was the second weekend.

I told Bill, "I can't miss Jody's wedding; she is my niece; she is my Godchild. My family will not understand."

He replied with, "Just think about this and pray about it."

That is when I asked, "Pray about it; what do you mean?"

"That is the way you get direction."

"Really?" I had never thought about prayer like that before. I remember thanking God; and I remember asking in the dire depths, "please, please" – that kind of thing.

I had heard about talking to God and asking for guidance to send the Holy Spirit to me, or show me what to do. But I had not lived that way.

Bill is not what I would call outwardly religious. But the Word of God is in him –he just lives it by his life and the way he treats people and listens to them. I guess I was really listening to him that day. Have I mentioned that Bill was a gift to me from God?

The weekend came for Bill to go to Cursillos. When he came home he said, "Linda, I can't tell you what goes on at the weekend, but I can tell you this – I have had Christ in my life and in my heart now for many, many years; but He is so full in my heart now that I feel like I am busting!" Then he proceeded to say, " You and I need to pray together."

"Together?" we had never done that before.

Bill prayed, "Lord, please come to her and make her know that this is something that she needs in her life. I want this so badly for her Lord. Help her make this decision to go to Cursillos."

The next thing I knew I was saying to my pastor, "OK, I'm going on the weekend, but I don't know that I am staying Saturday night." That is when the wedding was.

He said, "Oh, pray on that one."

"What? Pray on that?" I replied flippantly, "You mean I can actually get answers about Saturday night?"

Well, I went to Cursillos. I think it was more because Bill wanted it for me. I don't know that I heard instructions from the Lord to go. Saturday night was the night of the wedding, and I was actually scared about not going to this family event. However, the time came; and we were escorted to dinner. I can truly say that I had dinner with the Lord that Saturday night at Cursillos. (We aren't really supposed to share what happens at a weekend because it could spoil it for others who go. But it is a spiritual experience that builds to Saturday night.) On Sunday we each had to stand up in front and give a short talk about what the weekend had meant to us.

After thinking about it, I simply said, "I can't say how this weekend is going to change my life; I can't say right now. I can't see it; I can't see it yet. But I know that it has to because when I came into this, my heart was hard as stone; and this weekend it has been softened."

I would like to share with you a few "lightening bolts" that I experienced while at the retreat. "Let go and Let God." I had always tried harder to be in control when I would come to a place where I was out of control. Now, I work at "Letting Go and Letting God."

I learned that it is OK to be in the baby steps of faith. God loves me just the way I am, but he loves me too much to leave me that way! This is what I was looking for – sinner that I knew myself to be.

It was a gradual walk, after accepting Jesus in my heart and realizing that there was something much better for me. God doesn't just expect that I should know He is in my heart; He expects that I should live it and then do something for Him. Now that my heart is softening and I am open, "I see the light," so to speak. God has been with me all along, but I was too closed and too stubborn to open my heart and my eyes. I had no need to feel alone – what a pity!

I married Bill when I was 39, and I went to Cursillos when I was 54. At that point I was still in the dark even though I went to and was active in the church. Eventually, I volunteered to be Treasurer of the church we belonged to. Bill told me not to do it because he didn't think I was strong enough and because he'd had some bad experiences with the "people of the church." I volunteered anyway. I just didn't know where to go, where to find what I was needing – that personal relationship with Jesus. How do you make the walk? I would pick a place in the Bible and read it, but I still didn't get it. The road has been a fumbling and stumbling one. If someone had asked me if I was a Christian I would have said, "yes." You see, I didn't know what being a Christian meant; I really didn't. I had some good examples, but I just couldn't make it work. The job at the church gave me some good and some bad examples of Christian life.

Before I became a Christian, Jesus was a man who died for our sins – I didn't internalize it as my sins. It was a nice story. It wasn't that I didn't believe it was true – I did believe that it was true. But it didn't register. It didn't seem like a workable, useable piece of knowledge. When something goes wrong in your life, you use the tools that you have to fix it, to change it, or whatever you have to do to make it right again. Jesus was not a workable tool for me!

God's patience is wonderful. So, now I wonder – what am I going to do with this new faith that I have? I do share with my daughters that the biggest pain I have in my life is that I didn't lead them to a relationship with God. I had no God I could give them when they were growing up; however, I did have them Baptized. When I married Bill, he insisted that Melissa take Confirmation instruction; and she was confirmed – Dawn has never been confirmed. She's following in my footsteps and doesn't take her children to church. My mother sent us to Sunday School; but she had 7 children, and she wanted us out of the house. She never went to church. I knew all of the old songs. I still go to church and see people there like me who sing the songs; they know the words – I do not mean to be judgmental. I am just trying to show where I was and where I am now. I know what it feels like with and without Jesus in my heart.

Before having Christ in my life, I got through troubles by being hard, tough, capable, strong – it's the loneliest thing in the world. In fact, I recently had a conversation with my daughter, Dawn, about that. She said, "Mom I have always thought of you as capable and strong."

"Aaaaah!" I squealed and started to cry, " You know, I portrayed that I was capable and that I was strong; but there are times in your life when you need to be angry; you need to be sobbing; and you need to be in pain. You need to open up, and you need to share what's hurting you. I didn't do any of that, and I was hard to you girls; I was hard to you because that is how I needed to be. It's like a regiment, and it's how I got through life. I am still capable and strong, but now I ask for God's guidance."

As a hospice nurse, I had cared for Bill's first wife, Carlene. She was dying of colon cancer and could no longer give to him. He still loved her, hugged her, and teased her. I was given a peek at what marriage could be. She was dying – she had a loving husband and children. God was full in her heart. Carlene trusted that God would cure her.

How could there be a God? Why was He taking this wonderful woman with everything to live for and leaving me? Carlene actually became a caretaker to me. I was supposed to be the caregiver. She was in pain; yet, she was able to see my pain. I had no faith, no loving husband, no reason for life. She said to me many times. "God knows – he has the reason. Trust." I know that I am seeing her again someday. At her funeral a couple of her friends came up and said to me, "I want you to tell me the truth because I need to know this. Did she walk with the Lord to the end?'

I replied, "You know, she was a human being; she stumbled a little; but she was right with Him in the end. She was right with Him having faith that this was all right."

Kay, you know that I have recently lost my mom. There are parallels with her life and mine. We were so much the same. She was hard too. During the last two years of her life, Jody, a gal at the Senior

Citizens home where Mom was living, chipped away at her hard heart. Jody would invite Mom to do something, and Mom would tell her that she was just fine and wanted to stay in her room. Jody would always tell her that she would be back. Jody continued to befriend her. Mom had seven children and only my sister, Robin, wouldn't give up on her. Then somehow I saw my mom differently, and I changed. I decided that I wouldn't give up either. My mom became a giving person. She too had feared not being strong and capable. I know now that it was the Lord giving me a gift. She knew her Lord when she died – her heart had changed. I tried to witness to my brothers and sisters about the change in Mom, but then I remembered that God had been trying to get to me for years. I had not paid attention; so I needed to have patience. The last two years of my mother's life were a gift from God.

I have trust in the words of Jesus. I am not concerned about heaven. I need to be concerned about planting the seed so others can get on the right track. I don't think it is any different than getting a college education. It just isn't! You have to study the Word; you have to witness; you have to have a mission; you have to have discipline; God requires that.

When I got frustrated about some work I wanted to accomplish at church, my pastor consoled me by saying, "First of all you have to care, really care; then you have to ask; then you have to serve." I always go back to the patience of God. I remember how patient He is with me.

I took a prayer class with my sister, Robin, when my mother was very ill. I would drive the three and half-hours to the city to visit Mom and then go with Robin to the Prayer Class each week. As a result, I wrote to each of my girls – Dawn and Melissa; and also Kjirsten and Leslie (who were born to Carlene and Bill). I shared with them that I pray for them from *Ephesians 1:16-17 LBP*, "I have never stopped thanking God for you. I pray for you constantly, asking God, the glorious Father of our Lord Jesus Christ, to give you wisdom to see clearly and really understand who Christ is and all that he has done for you." And verse 19 reads, "I pray that you will begin to understand how incredibly great his power is to help those who believe him."

Epheisans 1:11a LBP also touches my heart, "Moreover, because of what Christ has done we have become gifts to God that he delights in..."

Do you know what it feels like to have somebody delight in you? It's like watching your Son and his wife with their baby. They delight in her. They glow, and their eyes sparkle when she does something cute. That's delight! When I think about the Lord delighting in me, I could conquer the world. I want my girls to know that too.

After reading *Ephesians 2:8 LBP*, I started using the word 'trust' instead of faith. It reads, "Because of kindness you have been saved through trusting Christ. And even trusting is not of yourselves; it, too, is a gift from God." We just have to trust, it doesn't have to be rocket science – it just doesn't. Like my pastor said, on a recent Sunday, "Genesis isn't science; Genesis is God; we don't have to prove or disprove anything. We just have to trust that however God did it, He did it."

Sometimes, I think the "faith" word is manipulated: Do you believe in this? Do you believe in that? You can't go to heaven if you believe that way. It is a problem for people who are stumbling and searching when Christians come across as knowing it all rather than loving and caring. However, I can get a handle on trust – just trust.

God had been trying to give me the gift of salvation for years, and I had not been accepting it. *1 Thessalonians 5:18 LBP* reads, "No matter what happens, always be thankful, for this is God's will for you who belong to Christ Jesus." Being thankful no matter what happens is really tough, but this verse has been very helpful. My friend whose husband was in jail sobbed and cried to God, "Why? Why?" One night her husband called her and said that he had had the opportunity to share Christ with another inmate that was going to kill himself. He told his wife, that he talked with him all night and he had accepted Christ as his Savior. If my friend's husband had not been there that man might be dead. God loves that man and has plans for his life. I believe this verse.

I now believe what Carlene said. "Trust that God knows – He knows the reason. He sees all."

She was dying and she believed and she trusted.

I believe this verse. Now my prayer is to live it. I pray for the Holy Spirit to be near me. By His grace I will walk a better path. I have been crying and reliving some things. I have some regrets but mostly joy for the future. It has been a long walk, and I still have far to go. I take some backward steps, but now I know that God walks with me. I *trust* where He is leading me.

dw

The Spirit Intercedes

"In the same way, the Spirit helps us in our weakness. We do not know what we ought to pray for, but the Spirit himself intercedes for us with groans that words cannot express." *Romans 8:26*

When we are depressed, confused, worried, grieved, or just plain too mentally and physically exhausted to pray or to read our Bible, that's OK for a time. God knows and understands our needs. Our faith doesn't depend on our reaching for God. It is wonderful to know that we can just put our trust in our Heavenly Father. We can be assured that the Spirit is interceding and praying for us. We can be comforted knowing that the Spirit of God is praying in a manner that is far beyond that of words. He is holding us close and carrying us through our trials to a new day.

dw

Worry, I Worry!

I am a worrier. I worry about many things, but usually it is centered around the safety of my family. I expect Cy home from work usually somewhere between 5 and 6 PM. If it gets to be later and I haven't heard from him, I become obsessed with looking out the window; my prayers turn to pleading, "Please help Cy call or come home soon – bring him here safely." I don't pray this just once; it plays over and over in my head. Then my stomach starts turning; and if too much time goes by, I find myself getting sick.

When the kids were teenagers, we had our pastor over one night to discuss this. We had a rule that if they couldn't be home when we expected them to be, they were to call home. Generally speaking they were pretty good about it. However, when there was a slip-up or some other reason the call was not made, I was a basket case. So, we needed to discuss this as a family with an outsider who could give some caring advise. I was at a place where I knew I couldn't go on the way I was, but I also knew that I didn't know how to control it. I often felt swallowed by the "Deep Woods" of fear and worry.

The purpose of our meeting was for my family to understand that my staying up at night for the kids, calling friends to check on them, and many tears was not just a sympathy play, but rather a very real condition that could eventually cripple how I functioned. As a result of our meeting with our pastor, my family became more considerate of me; and I tried to deal with my worrying nature rather than just berate myself for it or question my faith. I had been told that fear and faith could not abide together. However, that was very destructive for me because I knew that I had faith in God or I wouldn't have made it this far. Yet, fear and worry still plagued me much too often.

There was, in my mind, a good basis for this worry. By this time we had already experienced many losses. My brother had not returned home one evening, and it was morning before it was discovered that he had lost his life in a car accident. We had lost a young son, and I could not imagine surviving the pain of losing another child. We lived in a city where violence was not a stranger. Even though I knew that I could not live in constant fear, the memory of past pain clicked in; and I could no longer control my mind. I had brought this to my Lord in prayer countless times; one time I was reminded of the Apostle Paul. In *2 Corinthians 12:7-9*, he tells about a thorn given him in the flesh that he had asked the Lord to take away; but the Lord's answer was, "My grace is sufficient for you, for my power is made perfect in weakness." We have no idea what the "thorn" was. It was probably a physical malady of some sort, flesh being interpreted to mean body or because the mind is part of our body; perhaps it was some kind of emotional conflict. I had prayed about this many times, and through the years I learned how to talk more positively and reason with myself. This has been an enormous help. However, I now claim the promise that God's grace is sufficient and that my most bothersome weakness seems to be that of worry; so I trust that with God's power I will work through this.

We all worry to some extent. It is a real state of mind. It can come upon a person totally overtaking his/her thoughts to the point where it can impede all other activities. Worry comes hand in hand with stress. I don't see how worry can be present without causing intense stress. We all know how unhealthy stress is for us.

Worry usually starts with a very legitimate concern. We must be concerned for one another and bring those concerns to God in prayer. Becoming a prayer warrior is part of being a Christian. Genuine concern can help us make intelligent decisions and also can prompt us to care for one another. But with me there often comes the time when concern becomes worry and worry becomes real fear. When that happens it is nearly, if not totally, out of my control. My head knows that most often all the energy I am spending on worrying is, thank God, a big waste of time and needless stress. But somehow my emotions and my body get involved, and my head doesn't have a fighting chance of calming me down.

I have found that there are some very practical things I can do to help reduce this stress in my life. When the children were at home, I was very adamant that every member of my family always carry ID.

Even when we went on vacations, I made up cards for our pockets or purses that always had the address, phone number and dates of the places we were staying whether a motel or a residence. Now that we usually travel only as a couple, we still do this. This procedure gives me peace of mind. I also no longer apologize for calling to check on someone. It may be a little inconvenient for my husband; but he knows that if it helps my worry/stress level, it's worth it. If one of us leaves home and the other one is also gone, we are to leave a note stating where we are. We also have a telephone answering machine so messages can be left very easily.

I have taken comfort from the poem by Reinhold Niebhor -
"God grant me the serenity
to accept the things I cannot change,
the courage to change the things I can;
and the wisdom to know the difference."

"Accept the things I cannot change" – Many things, especially with adult children, are totally out of my control to change. I may not like all the choices they make, but I can look for something positive and be thankful for that. I am often reminded of the Apostle Paul's words in his letter to the *Philippians 4:8*, "Finally, brothers, whatever is true, whatever is noble, whatever is right, whatever is pure, whatever is lovely, whatever is admirable – if there is any excellent or praiseworthy – think about such things. There is always something wonderful to find and something to be grateful about. I know that when I worry, I lose my sense of being realistic. Normal delays can happen that are no fault of the person I am worrying about. I cannot change it, but neither can that person. So I tell myself to slow down, pray about it, and get busy with something to pass the time as quickly as possible. And when that doesn't work, I allow myself to sit by the window or the phone and wait.

"Courage to change the things I can" – Sometimes it takes courage to make phone calls because I know that I may bother the person I am worried about; however, that is something I can do, and at least I'll know that person is OK. A conversation with a family member or a friend about an issue that is bothersome to me may take a fair amount of courage, but in the end it can reduce the worry/stress level significantly. It takes courage to face others with concerns you may have about them. But, on the other hand, that conversation could be a positive factor in their life. Love is not always easy. Doing or saying the loving thing often takes much courage.

And the greatest challenge of all – "The wisdom to know the difference." The dictionary defines wisdom as, "Understanding of what is true, right, or lasting. Common sense; good judgment." That tells me that wisdom is something that may take time to discern. A decision may not come easily or quickly. Patience may be necessary to discover all the facts. In the end we may find that we just have to accept a situation even though we do not approve of it. Knowing what is within my power to change and what is out of my control is in itself a relief.

Controlling worry is still a struggle for me although I don't feel guilty about it anymore. At this point and throughout my life, it has been a part of who I am. The older I get, the more I know that God's grace is always sufficient for me. Not that I would choose to have this weakness, but I also know that I probably call on God much more in prayer because I do have it. Should the day come when God chooses to release me from unreasonable worry, I will praise and thank Him. If this is to be my thorn in the flesh for this life on earth, I will journey through this "Deep Woods" too, holding God's hand and knowing his Grace is always there for me.

dw

God's Hugs

"God hugs you. You are encircled by the arms of the mystery of God." – Hildegard Binges

Let's think about hugs. We usually either like them, take them for granted; or for one reason or another, we try to avoid them. I like to be hugged. It gives me a wonderful feeling of acceptance and security. I also like to give hugs. It is one way that I say, "I care about you!" Some of us are more ready and free to give hugs than others. It comes easy to us and is a sincere way of greeting, comforting, celebrating and saying, "Goodbye."

Hugs give hope. They warm and bring nourishment to the soul. There are times when I have felt that I have truly received a hug from God. A hug from God is usually unexpected – something out-of-the-blue. I believe that God uses us as His instruments to be at the right time and the right place to deliver His hug.

"So," you say, "What forms do God's hugs come in?"

A special time comes to my mind. Our Marine son, Kevin, was about to leave to serve in the Gulf War in 1991. His last phone call home before leaving was truly a time that I didn't want to end.

"Kevin," I said, "I feel confident that you are right with God."

He assured me, "Mom, please don't worry about that. I know where I will be if something should happen; and I will see you again."

Later when I was talking with a friend, I relayed to her how I felt that Kevin's simple statement of faith was a hug from God.

A phone call from a son, daughter, spouse or friend, at a time when it is so needed, is a hug from that person; but the timing is a hug from God.

A special scripture passage at a crucial time that speaks so particularly to me is an embrace from God.

God hugs us by blessing our efforts. When we sit back, we can realize how everything works together for good *Romans 8:28*.

When an idea or a word of re-assurance pops into our minds, it seems as though God is very close.

A moment of solitude – a time away from life's schedules and stress – can feel like being in God's arms and resting there.

The birds that sing, the leaves on the trees that rustle, flowers that bloom into seas of color, the ocean waves that come and go in unending rhythm, seasons that rotate, stars that majestically shine and the rains that nourish the earth are all hugs from God.

You can make your own list. The next time you share one of your hugs, in whatever form it may be, it could be the time the recipient will feel it was a hug from God.

dw

I Love You, Dad

As your son or daughter leaves for school, your child pauses, turns around, looks up at you and says, "I love you, Dad."

Your heart is suddenly filled with unspeakable joy; maybe tears fill your eyes and the cares of the day ahead melt away. You smile and with all the warmth and feeling that you can muster you reply, "I love you too!!"

The words, "I love you" must be the most healing words ever spoken. I believe that they can bring more joy and deliver the feeling of "life is good" more clearly than any other words spoken.

There is one Father of us all who would delight in hearing those words. After all He created us; He knows our needs; and He loves us more than any parent has or ever could.

The next time that you pray you just may want to say to your Heavenly Dad, "I love you."

dw

Just Love

Love. What a precious word! Love. What an intriguing concept! Love. God's love. God loves you. God loves me. At times it seems that the world just doesn't get it. God loved the world so much that He gave His only Son. His *only* son – for me – for you – for us!

God loves His creation. He loves us so much that He knows us by name. *Ephesians 4:15* tells us that the Father has named everyone in heaven and on earth. My heart fills as I ponder that I am God's child, and He knows me by name. I am even more awed when I read that He delights in me. The word delight is full of love. When something or someone delights in us, our faces light up and our smiles reach to our souls.

We were created with love; we were saved by love; and our response is to love. I *Timothy 1:5 RSV* reads, "...whereas the aim of our charge is love that issues from a pure heart and a good conscience and sincere faith." We are clearly charged to love.

God's love goes even further. He calls us His friends. We know how wonderful it is to have good friends – to be God's friend – to know that He claims us as His child. Now I am overwhelmed!

We were created with love; we are known by name; He delights in us; and by His grace we are saved through the death and resurrection of His only Son taking our place on the cross. When we realize and accept those facts, our hearts can't help but be filled with "God Love" that spills out in our love and caring for others.

Just love even when it's difficult and seemingly impossible. Reach to God, and let Him fill your heart once again with love that overflows to all of His children who are in our lives.

dw

Chapter Six

Memories
Along Our Way

Memories, sweet memories—
let us store them in our hearts
and take them out on occasion
to delight in and savor.

I Remember You, Leah

Leah, you were only nineteen when you went to be with Jesus. Only nineteen! It's such a short life! You seemed to have so much going for you and so much ahead of you. You wanted to be in some kind of ministry for Jesus. You had already spent several years doing that, even traveling to Ireland with Youth for Christ.

You were so full of life and fun. I heard how you were a force to be dealt with on the basketball court. The picture we have of you during a game tells the story. You also loved music; you put your heart into everything that you did. You were involved with life to its fullest.

I remember your laugh. I remember your sense of humor when I would call and mistake you for your sister, Elizabeth. You would just let me go on believing that you were she until I figured it out myself, and we then would laugh together. I remember how you didn't just call us Kay and Cy; you called us Aunt Kay and Uncle Cy, a special designation that I now treasure. I would never forget your birthday because it was the same day as our daughter's. You were exactly ten years younger than your cousin Kimberly. I remember the joy that my mother and father (your grandparents) felt when you were born.

Yes, you were just nineteen when you went to be with Grandma and Grandpa, Uncle Mark, and Cousin Kyle. As your aunt, it seems to me that the complications from the brain cancer that attacked you ended your life much too early.

I have learned that your life made such an impression on several people that some very special things are happening. When I was standing with your Dad at the hospital during our vigil with you that last night, your doctor told us that because of your spirit and witness to everyone that last year, a support group was being started for people with brain cancer.

At your Memorial Service, your school administrator, Dr. Harris, shared that he had always believed that Leah would make a big difference for Christ in the world. He went on to say that a scholarship fund had been set up for men and women who choose to go into the ministry. When your sister, Liz, graduated that following Spring, one of those Scholarships was awarded. So, during your short life, Leah, you made more of a difference for Christ than many do who live long lives.

Our consolation is that we know you knew Jesus. In your last days your family sensed that you were surrounded by ministering angels. You left this life with as much dignity and love and grace as you had lived life itself. You will always be with us, Leah. We will always remember you.

I love you,
Aunt Kay

dw

Leah Loving Music

A Woman of Faith

I really didn't know her for a very long time. In fact it was less than two years. Her first name was the same as my mother's. It was Esther – "Star" is one meaning of her name. This lovely lady became my mother-in-law.

She graciously welcomed me as her son's girlfriend and a short time later as his fiancé. She made me feel like I was the best thing that ever happened to her son. She was so excited about meeting my family and about our marriage. The two Esthers connected right away; and I realized, rather quickly, that she was a very gracious lady whom many people counted on as their friend.

She liked to entertain people and to laugh with them. There were always homemade treats to serve with a cup of coffee at a minute's notice. I learned that she was a very good listener, and friends knew they could confide in her.

Her church was important to her, and she was involved with the Ladies organization. My husband said that there was never a question about where they would be on Sunday mornings. Church and Sunday School were just a part of growing up. I was informed that her favorite hymn was *In The Garden*. I can easily understand that because I know she knew that "He" talked with her, and she knew that she was "His" own.

Cy also told me about how she was his biggest fan when he was a high school wrestler – she wouldn't miss a meet. When I met her, I knew immediately how important her children were to her.

One of her favorite sayings was, "Oh, you guys!" It was what she said when she learned that we were going to have a baby. This time, though, it was hard for her to say even that. You see, her life was ending at that point. We had been married about ten months. Just a couple of months later she died with her daughter at her bedside.

This special woman's faith became even more apparent to me the day of her funeral. The service was really a celebration of her life. I heard story after story about how much her presence in the church and community would be missed. I heard people talk about their times with Esther and how they appreciated her hospitality and her friendship. Esther was certainly a "star" to many people in that small town and surrounding area.

I remember being struck by how the service for one of God's saints was so filled with hope amidst the grief of a great loss. My mother-in-law's faith had impacted many people, and she would be greatly missed. She lived a life of faith and left her legacy of having walked with her God. That day her life was celebrated, and there was no doubt that she was now in her Heavenly Father's presence.

dw

A Random Act of Kindness
Memorials for Michael

It was late afternoon on the last Sunday in June. There had been people, mostly relatives, in and out for the last couple of days. Our hearts were once again broken; our eyes were often teary; and our minds were at times numb while, at other times, literally racing. Our 39 year-old nephew had died early on the Wednesday morning before. Any death of a dear one is sad. But, some deaths are especially tragic and can be extra hard to understand and to accept.

Michael was Cy's sister's only son. He was a handsome; personable man in his late 30's. We were always thrilled when Michael could make it to family gatherings. He had been through many struggles in his life including addiction. However, he seemed to be doing quite well once again with hopes and dreams for the future. Then one day that all changed.

Again, another child in our family had died. Cy's sister, Twilia, was on the road with the other parents whose children were taken in death. We knew that road well. We grieved for her and with her. Michael also had two children who needed him in their lives, as well as a sister who would miss him terribly. Added to Twilia's grief was the fact that Michael had not been "bad enough" for help from a Christian treatment center. She was a volunteer there and had asked for help for her son. Because of her disappointment with the Center, you would think that she would have quit volunteering after Michael's death – not Twilia. She continued to work with that Center to make its ministry an even better one.

Our home became a type of clearinghouse for messages and advice. That was fine. I always felt better being useful at times like these rather than just sitting and wishing that I could be helpful. At 4:00 on Sunday afternoon, I suggested to Cy that since everyone was gone for a time we should to go to a local florist to choose a gift from us and also one from some relatives in Iowa. So we left as the skies were threatening rain and closing time was fast approaching.

The shopping experience was a bit frustrating as it was hard to find help, and it was really hard to make up our minds about what we really wanted to get as memorials. Finally, the small evergreen tree (symbolizing eternal life) was decided upon; that the relatives from Iowa had requested, and a nice artificial tree was chosen for us to give to Twilia for her office.

We got to the checkout counter just as the doors of the florist were closing. I was asked to choose coverings for the pots and to write out instructions for delivery to the church. I felt like my brain had gone numb; I couldn't think and the tears started flowing down my cheeks so fast that I could barely see. My checkout clerk was in a bit of a hurry to close, and I was doing all that I could to not fall completely apart. Another clerk, about my age, noticed me and came over to me saying, "I think that you've been given a lot of responsibility; and it's a really tough time, isn't it?" I told her that my nephew had been tragically killed. She started helping me fill out of the cards needed, choose pot coverings, write out delivery directions, etc. She didn't hurry me at all. Finally, everything was paid for; and I was ready to leave. She then came around the counter and said, "I think that you need a hug." I was in her arms in a split second, letting an entire stranger comfort me. As I left, I thanked her for her patience and understanding.

On the way to our car, I shared with Cy how much this dear lady's random act of kindness had meant to me. The strength that she gave me stayed with me for the days to come. Even though I do not know her name, I will never forget her. Her kindness reminded me of how important my random acts of kindness can be to someone else in need.

dw

I Jesu Navn

Grandpa Bjerke always prayed the table prayer when the family was together for meals. He was also asked to pray it at his granddaughters' wedding receptions and often for other family events. However, many of us present didn't understand the words because Grandpa prayed this prayer in Norwegian.

> I Jesu naven gír vi til bords
>   Í spise, drikke pí ditt ord.
> Deg, Gud til ére, oss til gavn,
> Sí Fír vi mat i Jesu navn
> Amen.
> English Translation
> In Jesus' name to the table we go
> To eat and drink according to His word.
> To God the honor, us the gain,
> So we have good in Jesus' name.
> Amen.

We seldom hear that prayer because no one can pray it quite like Grandpa Bjerke did. It is nice to hold the memory of Cy's Dad and our children's Grandfather as the one who thanked God for our food in his native tongue.

I have another memory of my father-in-law: He was a hummer. He just hummed tunes to himself; they were barely audible to the rest of us. The one I remember was a hymn I learned as a child, *If I Gained the World but Lost My Saviour.* When Cy and his brother, Bill, were recently together they talked about remembering their father humming that tune. I pray that our children too will one day have treasured spiritual memories about their mother and father.

dw

Grandma (Esther) and Grandpa (Bill) Bjerke

It's Good to Laugh

Laughter is food for the soul. Vitality permeates our whole body when we laugh. It's sad to think about the times that I have starved my soul – times when there just wasn't enough energy to laugh. The burdens I carried seemed to be so many and so heavy that laughter was only an elusive reality. Lighthearted, side splitting laughter of better times was only vaguely remembered.

"I just want to laugh!" were my words when I felt that I needed to get away. I wanted a vacation to do things that were silly and fun. Please, no phone calls, no one asking me if I could do a favor; if I knew where; if I had found; or if I could go. I could not deal with anymore demands or responsibilities. I wanted someone to take me away and make me laugh.

Sometimes laughter has to be restored with time. In the event of a sudden and very untimely death, the shock to the whole body is so tremendous that it takes time to heal enough to be able to laugh again. I am not talking about nervous laughter that often accompanies these times of stress and serves as an appropriate therapy in itself. I am referring to the spontaneous, genuine release of the positive emotion called laughter.

I remember leaving my parent's home after a weekend visit quite some time after the death of our son, Kyle. As we were driving away, Cy and I started laughing about something (I don't even remember what) – really laughing. Suddenly, I exclaimed, "This is the first time that we have really laughed since Kyle died, and it feels so good!"

It was such an important moment that I still remember it well. It took a long time for emotional health and energy to be restored enough so laughter could spill forth again.

Laughter is a wonderful gift from God, and it must be used. A sense of humor is essential to a healthy mind and body. Cultivate it; and consciously look for the funny things in this crazy, mixed-up world. Don't let laughter slip away and be forgotten in the maze of your daily routine. Even if you have to get away and have a change of scene for a few days, do it! Maybe you need to spend some time with good friends and laugh over silly things together.

Use this precious gift of laughter! Your life will be enriched and blessed. When you feel like you just want to laugh, it's time to make it happen.

dw

ChapterSeven

Light
In the Woods

The light brings us health, joy and wholeness.

I have been asked to address the subject of how God's will manifests itself in our lives. I'm not an educated theologian – just an experienced women who has given her life to Christ. So, I decided to write an analogy in story form about the subject. It helped me – I hope it speaks to you in some way too.

The Garden of Eden and God's Will

Conversations about "God's Will" have been present for centuries. Often within Christian circles we hear, "If it's God's Will, I'll do it."

"We'll have to accept this death because it was God's Will."

"By the Will of God."

"God's Will must have been to save Mark from some terrible tragedies that could have been in his future."

I ask, "What's more tragic than death?"

"We're waiting for God's Will," or certain and frank statements like, "We know it's God's Will, or "It is God's Will" are common.

In some respects I envy these people who seem to have such a clear connection to God that they absolutely know what "God's Will" is. Their lives must never become static or disconnected. They must be living so in tune that their messages from God are always clear and unscrambled. I have to confess that has not always been my experience. I also have a little trouble at times relating God's Will and my responsibility to use the common sense God has given me. If something goes wrong, am I to say, "It was God's Will and dismiss the event?" I usually look for my responsibility in what happened.

Could I have done something differently? My prayer may be, "Dear God, show me how I could have handled this situation with more wisdom so I can learn from it. Please forgive me, and continue to guide me and lead me." "Oh," you say, "You do believe in God's Will, after all." And I will reply to you, that I do – but in what seems to be a little more complicated, yet, in some respects, a really simplified way.

What happened to God's Will in the Garden of Eden? Picture it! A brand new garden with lush bushes, tall trees, a sparkling brook, beautiful flowers, colors everywhere. And in the middle of the garden stood two people – they didn't even wear the latest fashions. Their fresh, clean, new skin was all they needed. And God said, "It is good." A monkey probably swung from a tree, and a rabbit played under a bush as squirrels ran on a tree branch; or maybe a deer peered quietly at these two creatures as it stood under sun-lit blue skies wondering what their next move would be. It would certainly seem that God's supreme plan had been accomplished. God was no longer lonely, and His creation was flawless. It was truly a perfect world. Adam and Eve were not only created with strong physical bodies, but they were also given minds with thought processes that were very active.

In the beginning there was no sin in the world, but there was the potential for sin. God didn't create Adam and Eve as prisoners in this wonderful garden. They were created in "His" image – they were soon to learn all about choices.

Ahhh, choices. We all want the right to make choices. And God gave us that ability, but choices bring with it responsibility and consequences. So how do we make choices?   Let's go back to that Garden – Adam and Eve were soon going to have to start making choices. What we can't have always looks the most inviting. It was "human nature" in The Garden and it is human nature now. God commanded the man, saying, "You may eat freely of every tree of the garden; but of the tree of *Knowledge of Good and Evil* you shall not eat; for in the day that you eat of it, you shall die," Genesis 2:16-17. God named that tree – it was special. I think we are safe to assume that there wasn't static in God's communication lines in the beginning – his directions were quite clear.

Those apples must have looked so good to Eve. Apparently, Adam didn't bother to tell her about God's command. Then comes another player in this scene – Satan himself, disguised as one of God's creatures. The lowest of all the creatures – a serpent. For the life of me, I cannot imagine how Eve could have been taken in by that serpent. But she was – temptation invaded God's perfect world, and God didn't stop it. He let Eve make the choice. It wasn't His Will for her to eat the apple, but God didn't stop her. So there went perfection. Sin was in God's once perfect world, and another plan was needed. You see, God loved Adam and Eve. God's love is the ultimate love – never failing and unending. God still had hope for his newly created world. He loved the people He had created, and He wanted more of them. But now He knew that not all the people He created would love Him. Not all these people would live according to His Will. And there would have to be consequences for sin. Wow! Now this had become complicated. What was God to do?

The truth is that life is usually very complicated for each one of us. As Christians we have accepted Jesus in our hearts and live in God's Grace. Yes, grace bought by Jesus via the cross and hope for our future in eternity. God's Supreme Will for each of us is to live with Him in eternity. If we have accepted His Son in our lives, that Supreme Will does become a reality for each one of us. Even though that hope is what keeps us going and gives us real joy – we've got a world to live in. In that world there's all kinds of influences – many of them evil or at least certainly not to our benefit.

So, if God's Supreme Will is eternal life, how does His Will affect us here on earth? Does God have a plan for each one of us? If we give our life to Him, does God direct our lives?

I believe that when we are born into this world, God does see what would be perfect for our lives. He gives us talents and abilities to use in this life for His glory and for the good of others. God does not wish His children to suffer He only wants the best for us. So, we can assume since he created and knows each and every one of us, He does have a Supreme Will for us, just as He did for Adam and Eve.

Here we are back at that Garden again. A tempter enters our lives or the lives of someone close to us as it did Eve's, and our path is altered. Maybe it was something that we had no control over, but we are no longer in God's Supreme Will. We know that bad things do happen to Christians who are seeking God's Will. Are we then to say that God caused it? Am I to agree that God caused Mark's accident? Or that God caused birth defects in Kyle's body? Or that God gives young people cancer? I cannot agree to that reasoning! The God I know is a God of love and a Great God of Grace who loves His children more than any parent on earth could. Where does that leave us now?

Remember Eve had a choice. Often our choices don't affect us right away, but years later they can affect us and the people close to us. That's the world we live in because of a choice made in that first garden. Kyle's death was ultimately caused by birth defects. I didn't smoke, drink or abuse my body. But something in our combined genealogical make-up produced a wonderful child with a birth defect. God is almighty so He could have prevented it, right? I suppose so; however, it didn't work that way. Birth defects are a consequence of an imperfect world. They aren't a punishment – just a consequence.

Do I believe God caused Mark's car to run into that bridge, flip over on him and cause his death? No Way! Why would I believe that? One of two things likely happened. He was tired, fell asleep and loose dirt on the road grabbed the wheels of the car; that was it. Or, my dad felt that maybe he had a heart attack because Mark was born with a heart murmur. Regardless, it was the result of several things in the world we live in happening and causing a fatal accident. I do not believe that just because we are Christians there will be no accidents or other terrible events in our lives.

Our adopted Korean daughter, Kimberly, had to have a total hip replacement at the age of 21. She also had a birth defect. Her hip never developed because of severe malnutrition as an infant and the likely malnutrition of her birth mother. She suffered the consequences of neglect from years before. Did God plan that?

So, where was God when Mark died? He was right there beside us – crying with us – knowing how Mom and Dad felt because He too had a son die. He took this untimely death and worked with it to bless other people's lives. The fact is that circumstances caused Mark's death. But our loving God was there and worked in the hearts of people who knew Mark to bring them closer to Him. Adam and Eve sinned, but God sent His Son to redeem them and us. Mark died, but God was there and worked miracles through the tragedy to create good. And because I've chosen to write about this all these years later, I pray that God is still touching people. That is why I can hold on to what Paul says in *Romans 8:28*, "We know that in everything God works for good with those who love him, who are called according to his purpose." "But," you reply, "If God loves us so much, why does He allow us to suffer." Paul in the book of Romans says, that he prayed and prayed for the thorn in his flesh to be removed; however, as far as we know, God chose not to heal him on this earth. God spoke to the Apostle Paul; "My grace is sufficient for you, for my power is made perfect in weakness."

When our son, Kyle, was diagnosed, we were frantic parents trying to make sense out of the situation. We prayed for healing again and again and again. I started reading book after book – most of them stating that God meant us to be whole and healed, and all we needed was enough faith and persistence. We went to healing services with him; he was anointed and had the laying on of hands. Since he was a child, I was led to believe that if only I had enough faith he would be healed. After all, it was purely and simply, "God's Will." Wow, what a message! It was a message that eventually led to the near destruction of my faith.

Kyle was not healed here on earth. I do believe that, at times, physical healing occurs here on earth that cannot be explained in any other way than Divine. I have experienced that with both family and friends. But I also believe that my mistake was being led to believe that we must demand healing from God. After all, that's really what that kind of theology is – a demand. I'm convinced that God's Supreme will is a physically whole body for all of us. However, I am not convinced that the healing must take place in this life on earth.

A while after Kyle died, some friends of ours brought their son (Kyle's age) home from the hospital. Someone had made a banner for the dining room that read, "God said, 'Yes' to Nathan." That statement hit me like a rock, and I asked myself, "Does that mean that God said 'No' to Kyle?" By then my thinking had been straightened out and my faith strengthened enough so that my answer was, "God also said 'Yes' to Kyle." God healed Kyle in heaven, and now His Supreme Will for Kyle has been accomplished.

Answers aren't always quickly apparent. There's a process that must take place. Only God knows why it took so many years after "The Garden" before the "Cross and the Resurrection." However, God did have another plan, and it did call for a particular genealogy. It also called for a loss. It called for one of the greatest losses that can be experienced – the loss of a child. God willingly laid the sins of the world on His perfect Son, Jesus, and sacrificed Him so the rest of His children, you and me, could be saved. We are all God's children – just as Jesus is. Yet, it would take redemption to bring us back to God's perfection. It would mean that sin would have to be defeated. So, God's Son was born of a virgin and lived a sinless life on earth. Then, obediently, He gave His life for all of God's other children who had ever lived or ever would live. However, dying was not enough; redemption was completed when three days later life miraculously came back to Jesus. Now the work had been done. God's children could again live with Him in Eternity. The sin committed in the Garden of Eden had been paid for. God's Will had been accomplished.

Do you think of yourself as God's child? You are! Would God deliberately bring harm or evil to anyone of His Children? I don't believe so. Evil does not come from God. Evil is defined as – wickedness, injurious, harmful. If everything that happens to Christians is totally orchestrated by God, how do you explain it when a Christian woman is attacked or raped? How does one explain birth defects that come indiscriminately to both Christians and non-Christians? A drunk driver kills all the occupants of a car he hits, and a good Christian family is wiped out instantly. We look for answers.

One may say, "God has His reasons."

"No," I say, "I can't accept that." If I accept that, I also have to say that God had a reason for Eve to disobey. No way! Sin is simply a result of Eve's desire for something she shouldn't have. Bad things happen; we must accept that they happen as a result of evil. But God is bigger than evil; and he never gives up – He is always there – staying with His children in their hurt, recovery, grief and daily struggle to bring sense back to life. Eve sinned, but that wasn't the end. God's grace doesn't end and is there for all of us. When our life leads us through the "Deep Woods" at various times in our life, God is there with His strength and His love. His grace really is sufficient for us; and He will never, never leave us. God's Will is that we accept His Son's act of redemption and live our life in service. God's Supreme Will is that we live with Him for eternity. No evil will change that.

dw

LOVE IS –

Love is a hug and a smile,
Love is sitting together for awhile.
Love is a gift freely given,
Love is a glimpse of heaven.
Love holds on when things are tough,
Love makes smooth out of the rough.
Love fills with joy the heart,
Love keeps us close when apart.
Love was God's only Son,
Love was how victory over sin was won.

dw

Easter Day Every Day

Easter Sunday has little to do with bunnies, egg hunts or Easter bonnets for me – other than the fun that they bring. It does, however, have everything to do with new life.

Easter is Resurrection Day. After Maundy Thursday and the Last Supper, after Good Friday and the crucifixion, Resurrection Day brings victory. In *John 11:25-26 NIV* Jesus says, "I am the resurrection and the life; he who believes in me will live, even though he dies; and whoever lives and believes in me will never die." That is victory! He goes on to ask, "Do you believe this?"

No matter what trials, tribulations and sorrows that this life on earth brings us, there is ultimate victory for those who have accepted Jesus Christ as their Savior.

When the challenges come, as they certainly will, remember *Philippians 4:13*, "I can do all things through him who gives me strength." Surrendering our problems – indeed our whole life to Christ – gives us a freedom and a power and a peace that only God can give through His Son.

Every day is Easter Day because every day is a new start. I may have really messed up yesterday at work, with friends or with my family. I may have disappointed myself by something I did or did not do. When I went to bed I felt depressed, and probably disgusted. But guess what! I woke up in the morning to a new day and a new start!

Each day is a gift to be unwrapped and tenderly cared for. Pause for a moment and say outloud, "This is the day that the Lord has made; let us rejoice and be glad in it!"

Not every day is going to be a perfect day because we are not a perfect people. But we can trust by God's grace (even when it's almost impossible to believe) what Paul tells us in *Romans 8:28*, "We know that in everything God works for good with those who love him, who are called according to his purpose."

If you haven't taken that step of asking God for forgiveness and of giving your life to Christ, I am encouraging you to do just that. Then no matter what this life is throwing your way, or whatever is in your future, every day can be an Easter day for you.

dw

The Sun Will Shine Again

I heard a bird singing today
High on his perch in a tree.
His sweet song seemed to say,
"There's no happier creature than me."

That little bird's simple life
Can almost be envied by me.
There seems to be no worry or strife
Cluttering his little life needlessly.

So when the dark clouds come his way,
He trusts that his maker surely can
Provide his needs day by day,
Knowing that the sun will shine again.

Back Where I Began

I grew up in Wisconsin with the beautiful woods around me. I played in the shade of the big maple trees in our yard. I went to the pasture to get the cows, and I held my daddy's hand as we went into the "Deep Woods."

Cy and I were blessed to be able to purchase 11 acres of woods in Wisconsin a little more than an hour south of my childhood home. We cleared the land and built big garages for Cy and a home for us. I now sit in the shade of elms and oaks and sumac as I read, write and relax. We are almost retirement age, and this is where we will live for our remaining years.

I quietly watch with amazement as a Doe and her twin Fawns come into our yard and look around. I count the wild turkey as they parade through the edge of our lawn. We have vegetable and flower gardens in the summer. I love the fresh air and driving the country roads.

I have woods to walk in here too. My daddy isn't here to hold my hand, but I won't get lost now. I am back in Wisconsin, and I feel like I have come home.

Life hasn't been easy much of the time, but it's good to be alive at this moment. I know that there will be tough times ahead because that's just the way life is. And even if the day should come when I can't hold my husband's hand anymore and I feel the "Deep Woods" of loneliness surround me, I won't be alone. Life has assured me of one thing that will never fail – my Heavenly Father's hand is always reaching out beckoning me to grasp it. He will hold me tightly until the day we meet face to face where there is no weeping and no fear of being lost in the "Deep Woods." We are so blessed!

dw